The Emergent Christ

The Emergent Christ

Exploring the Meaning of Catholic in an Evolutionary Universe

Ilia Delio, OSF

ORBIS BOOKS

Maryknoll, New York 10545

Founded in 1970, Orbis Books endeavors to publish works that enlighten the mind, nourish the spirit, and challenge the conscience. The publishing arm of the Maryknoll Fathers & Brothers, Orbis seeks to explore the global dimensions of the Christian faith and mission, to invite dialogue with diverse cultures and religious traditions, and to serve the cause of reconciliation and peace. The books published reflect the views of their authors and do not represent the official position of the Maryknoll Society. To learn more about Maryknoll and Orbis Books, please visit our website at www.maryknollsociety.org.

Library of Congress Cataloging-in-Publication Data

Delio, Ilia.
    The emergent Christ : exploring the meaning of Catholic in an Evolutionary Universe / Ilia Delio.
        p. cm.
    Includes bibliographical references (p.   ).
    ISBN 978-1-57075-908-6 (pbk.)
    1. Evolution—Religious aspects—Catholic Church. 2. Jesus Christ—Person and offices. 3. Spirituality—Catholic Church. I. Title.
    BX1795.E85D75 2011
    248—dc22
                                                                2010032700

Place three grains of sand inside a vast cathedral, and the cathedral will be more closely packed with sand than space is with stars.

—James Jeans

The most incomprehensible thing about the universe is that it is comprehensible.

—Albert Einstein

The Earth and all that is in it belongs to the Whole, to be tended by all in co-operation with Love.

—Psalm 50, adapted by Nan Merrill

Contents

Introduction

In his *Tale of Two Cities* Charles Dickens penned the famous lines, "It was the best of times, it was the worst of times." How appropriate these words are for our own time in Catholic Christian life, which has become a chimera of reflections: for some the brightness of new life in the restoration of preconciliar practices and norms, and for others the darkness of a church in dissolution. I am not an ecclesiologist, so my task is not to examine the complexities of the church. However, as a theologian involved in the dialogue between science and religion, I wonder about the future of Christian life as it is unfolding in the present moment, a moment divided between scandal among the inner ranks of the church, a Vatican investigation of religious women, and a church struggling to grow amid the complexities of a globalized world. What is the church becoming? What is becoming of Christian life in this secular, postmodern age? I ponder these questions as I look out my window to the Holy Land Franciscan Monastery across the street, a replica of the Church of the Holy Sepulchre in Jerusalem. Every week bus loads of people visit the monastery and the various shrines that replicate the principal places of Jesus' life and death. Some are pilgrims and visit the monastery as a place of prayer and spiritual healing. Others are members of tour groups and wander around the monastery gardens as if they were in Versailles. For all visitors the monastery is a place of history and story, not unlike visiting the Smithsonian museums down the road. In both places, monastery and museum, history and story blend together and visitors wander about amid the ruins of civilizations that once flourished.

History, of course, is what we are all about—not just recent history but eons of history. Evolution is the history of the cosmos, the story of how biological life and cosmological life unfold. Evolution tells us that creatures are the result of billions of years of a meandering, haphazard process of "natural selection," a journey marked by untold pain and suffering, loss, waste, and in the end, extinction for most species. After billions of years of evolution, it is a testament to divine love that we are here. Teilhard de Chardin described evolution as a "biological ascent" from matter to spirit, a movement toward more complex life forms. At critical points in the evolutionary process, qualitative differences emerge. "There is only one real evolution," he said, "the evolution of convergence, because it alone is positive and creative."[1] Although some people see the process of evolution as a meaningless process suffused with blind chance, the dynamic nature of the universe speaks to us, from a Christian perspective, of the home in which a loving Creator has placed us. The gift of Darwin's science to theology, John Haught claims, is that it can give depth and richness to our sense of the great mystery of religion.[2] Indeed, the science of evolution helps open up new windows of insight to the God-world relationship whereby we see creation not as a static world but as a relationship between the dynamic being of God and a world in process of coming to be. The openness of the cosmos to what is new, its capacity to leap forward, the emergence of intelligent beings, all direct the believer to the nature of the divine presence empowering the whole cosmic process. The whole creation, with humanity as its growing tip, emerges from an evolutionary process, exists in evolution, and develops through convergence and complexity.

Evolution shows us that change is integral to new life. Given a sufficient amount of time, life evolves. To evolve is not only to change but to become more complex, to unite in such a way that new forms of life emerge and diverge. The key to evolution is openness to the environment. Open systems can be influenced by the environment and change in relation to the environment. Closed systems cannot evolve, because they cannot be influenced by the environment; thus they seek to preserve their resources within. The systems theorist Erich Jantsch wrote that "to live in an evolutionary spirit means to engage with full ambition and without any reserve in the structure of the present, and yet to let go and flow into a new structure when the right time has come."[3] Do we as Christians live with an evolutionary spirit? It is my belief we do not; rather, we live in two world systems. In our everyday world we are open to the changes of culture in consumerism and technological progress (we have no problem keeping up with the latest technological gadgets), but in our theology and ecclesiology we live in the closed system of a pre-scientific, medieval church, the world of Plato, Aristotle, Dionysius, and Thomas. On the whole we Christians are more comfortable with scholastic thought and Aristotelian philosophy than with process theology or chaos theory.

Jesuit scientist and mystic Pierre Teilhard de Chardin was suspicious that Christianity makes its followers inhuman—that it becomes a series of rote doctrines devoid of life, pointing believers to a starry heaven away from the world. Christians are not conscious of their divine responsibilities, he claimed, but see Christian life as a series of observances and obligations, not the realization of the soul's immense power.[4] This leads to a static Christianity, a mechanization of Christian life whereby the language, symbols, and metaphors of theology and ecclesial life resist growth and change. As a result Teilhard said, Christians lose consciousness of their divine responsibility, which, in his view, is to evolve. Evolution, he said, is what Christianity is about; the whole development of life to mind, matter to spirit, is the genesis of Christ. This idea comes as a shock to many people for whom the title Christ belongs to the name Jesus almost as a surname. To think of Christ in terms of evolution seems scandalous—and perhaps it is scandalous—but not the scandal of heresy; rather, it is the scandal of divine love. Unless we know God as love, we cannot know the Christ as source and goal of an evolutionary universe. Hence, one aim of this book is to illuminate the God of scandalous love who is in evolution. Russian philosopher N. Berdyaev saw a contradiction between our view of personal perfection and our interpretation of divine perfection. While we may see God as self-sufficient, immobile, and uncompromisingly demanding, he said, we consider these attributes despicable in humans.[5] Berdyaev's insight to God captures the heart of my explorations on evolution and divine mystery. He writes: "People are afraid to ascribe movement to God, because movement indicates the lack of something, or the need for something that is not there. But it may equally well be said that immobility is an imperfection, for it implies the lack of the dynamic quality of life."[6] Evolution reflects dynamic life, as matter evolves to spirit. The emergent Christ in evolution is not only the process of divine-created unfolding life but the evolution of God as well.

To speak of God in evolution adds a new dimension to Saint Paul's insight that all creation groans aloud the pangs of new birth (Rom 8:22). What is this new birth that we await? Is Christ the hope for all creation in union with God? What does this mean for us and the cosmos? My explorations of Christ in evolution lead me to suggest that love is *the* metaphor of Christ and that divine love incarnating evolution is the work of the Spirit. To be engaged in the mystery of Christ is to be caught up in the Spirit of new life, creativity, imagination, and openness to the future. Spirit incarnating matter is energy for a new future. When we fail to see the spiritualization of matter and its openness to new life, we wind up in a split-level universe aiming for new life on a different ontological level, as if matter itself may dissolve into spirit. We still bear the weight of Neoplatonism with its otherworldly ascent to a higher realm. The Neoplatonic ladder of ascent is a movement away from, and rising above natural, sensible things as though they were inferior and in some sense, not real.[7] The emphasis of spirit over matter diminishes the natural goodness of the created world. Neoplatonists believed that the created world should motivate one to turn inward in the search for God and scale the metaphysical ladder to the spiritual and divine realms by means of universal concepts.[8]

Teilhard realized that the Greek metaphysical structure supporting Christian doctrine was too static for the dynamic world of evolution, as science describes it. He suggested that we need a new metaphysics fitting to the world as we now know it. Whereas in the past the Creator was structurally independent of the creation, in an evolving world God is not conceivable other than being confluent with the process of cosmogenesis.[9] The notion of God in the midst of the cosmogenic process provides a metaphysical basis to the concept of emergence in nature. Emergence points to the appearance of novel structures or forms in evolution. New things happen, and they are different from what already exists or has existed. If emergence describes the way nature evolves, what does it say about God? Can we understand the Trinity as an infinite emergent process? In this respect, change is not contrary to God; rather, change is integral to God because God is love and love is constantly transcending itself toward greater union. By change I do not mean God becomes something other than God; rather, God is a continuous becoming in love because of the absolute dynamism of divine love. Contrary to classical belief in God's immutability, it is because God can change that God is absolute love and hence ever faithful in love. The dynamic life of the Trinity as ever newness in love means that every divine relationship is a new beginning because every divine person is a transcendent horizon of love. Being is transcendence in love, and God's Being in love is eternally free.

Only when we see God as newness in love can we speak of God in relationship to an evolutionary creation, not as cause and effect but as novelty and future, the *plenum* of divine imaginaries. God is the horizon, the future who calls us into being, and the inner source of our becoming. God creates from the future out of the ever newness in love that is always more than the present moment can hold. Creation therefore thrives on the threshold of the future endowed with freedom, promise, and openness to new life. Contrary to the classic notion of Godhead (and hence metaphysics), creation does not return to its source; rather, creation moves forward, driven by the power of love into an ever new horizon of love. Christ is the symbol of creation's future in God, a future of newness in love, and our hope that love alone will endure. Hence, the twofold purpose of this book is to explore Christ as the future of our becoming and the role of Christian life in relation to the emergent Christ. By the *emergent* Christ I mean the novel appearance of God incarnate through a complexity of factors that includes spiritual conversion, prayer, and agapic love, which can lead to new relationships. Evolution, as Teilhard indicated, is the process of birthing the Christ within through a progression of unifying relationships and greater complexity; that is, the whole evolution is intended to become the fullness of Christ. Emergence means that the appearance of Christ in evolution is always a new event, a new relatedness, in such a way that Christ is always the future horizon of the cosmos.

As I began work on this book, my colleague John Haughey, SJ, published a book on Catholic higher education called *Where Is Knowing Going?* In this brilliant book on catholicity and the intellectual tradition, Haughey opened up for me a fresh, new meaning of the word *catholic* in a way faithful to the tradition and yet wholly new in content. He writes: "The term catholicity means openness and in contrast to what is incomplete and partial sectarian, factional, tribal and selective. . . . The word connotes movement towards universality or wholeness. . . . The dynamism of catholicity is toward a fullness it never possesses; it awaits a wholeness that beckons rather than materializes. . . . Catholicity is a heuristic that is never completed but remains an orientation, a drive and undertow that anticipates a transcendent entirety."[10] Haughey's insights into *catholic* liberate this word from layers of history that have enclosed it in a sealed-tight container, opening it up to its truest meaning as the very inner dynamic of an evolutionary universe. I have borrowed Haughey's renewal of the word *catholic* and have used it as a hermeneutic to describe Christian life in an evolutionary universe. To be catholic is to be a "whole maker," to unite what is separate, and thus to evolve toward greater unity. In this respect *catholic* and *Christ* belong together, even apart from their institutional synthesis. Creation as incarnation is the process of making whole; evolution itself can be described as the process of making wholes over long periods of time. The incarnation is the explicit making whole of divinity and humanity in the unity of person, without change, division, separation, or confusion. Haughey indicates throughout his book that catholicity has an inner dynamism. "Once the notion of catholicity becomes static," he writes, "it does not make a whole person, nor does it make a faith whole."[11] From my perspective, the dynamism of catholicity is the heart of the emergent Christ and Christian life in evolution.

To this end the book contains nine chapters (yes, it is *all* about Trinity!), beginning with the story of cosmic evolution, coursing through the meaning of God in evolution and the emergence of Christ, and concluding with new ways of seeing Christ in evolution. Although the story of the cosmos and the main aspects of the new science are now familiar to many readers, it is important to begin here because theology is a function of cosmology, that is, our understanding of the cosmos shapes our understanding of God. Creation is a fundamental book of revelation. The story of the Big Bang is the new Genesis story, one that is awesome, powerful, filled with goodness, and very old. It is important to tell the new cosmos story both to know our origin and to anticipate our future. Insights from evolution and quantum physics offer insights to created reality that help differentiate the God-world relationship from the classical metaphysics of Thomas and Bonaventure. Three insights from science today that shed light on the emergence of Christ are morphogenetic fields, quantum entanglement, and holons. Each of these discoveries points to the inherent relationality of the material universe and will be explored as new ways of understanding Christian life and participation in the reign of God.

Chapter 2 discusses God in evolution. In his book *Deeper than Darwin*, John Haught indicates that evolution requires a revolution in our thoughts about God because the whole cosmic process

is narrative to the core. "Traditional theology," he states, "has con-
ceived of God too much in terms of the notion of a Prime Mover
impelling things from the past."[12] In Haught's view, evolution is a
forward movement toward greater complexity and consciousness;
hence, it demands that we think of God as drawing the world from
"up ahead," attracting it forward into the future. The notion of
God as future was the principal focus of Teilhard de Chardin, who
asked, "Who will give evolution its own God?"[13] "Half a century
after Teilhard's death," Haught writes, "we have yet to answer this
question satisfactorily. For the most part, theologians still think
and write almost as though Darwin, Einstein and Hubble never
existed. . . . The natural world and its evolution remain distant from
dominant theological interest."[14] The search for a God of evolution is no small task, but it seems to me that without the God of an
evolutionary cosmos, theology becomes incredulous in the face of
science. To assume this task, I turn to two insightful thinkers of the
medieval period, Bonaventure and Meister Eckhart, to explore the
dynamic Trinity, in which change is essential to relationship. The
evolution of God is the God of ever newness in love.

Chapter 3 probes the integral relationship between creation and
incarnation, or the processes of evolution and creative union, as
Teilhard described them. Teilhard recognized that there is a unifying influence in the whole evolutionary process; evolution has direction. The ultimate mover of the entire cosmogenesis, he indicated, is something that is simultaneously *within* and *in front of* the
advancing wave of development, beckoning it, as its ideal culmination. Teilhard identified this prime mover with God. He described
Christ as the future fullness of the whole evolutionary process, the
"centrating principle" and "Omega point" where the individual and
collective adventure of humanity finds its end and fulfillment. Because incarnation is integral to evolution, the genesis of Christ in
evolution is always the emergence of new union or a unity of greater
complexity. Teilhard described the God of the future, the God "up
ahead," as the ultimate force of attraction for the universe, drawing
the universe toward intensification of complexity and new creation.

The use of *catholic* as a hermeneutic sheds new light on Jesus'
message of the reign of God as a new consciousness of being in the
world, one of relatedness, inclusivity, non-duality, and community.
Chapter 4 takes up the meaning of *catholic* as movement toward
wholeness and examines catholicity, first in the early church, and

then in Jesus of Nazareth. I examine Jesus' life and mission as one of "whole making." As the wellspring of divine love emerging from within, Jesus shows us what it means to be a human person and the way to deepen our humanity toward the fullness of life. Jesus' whole making is continued in Chapter 5, where I take up the central core of Christian faith, the resurrection. Here I discuss the power of the risen Lord as the power of new life for *this* creation. N. T. Wright's work on the resurrection is immensely helpful, and I look to Wright to dispel some of the myths of resurrection and to sharpen the lens on heaven as the goal of evolution in relation to God. The resurrection is not an otherworldly miracle but the glorification of humanity and hence earthly reality in God; it anticipates new life and a new future for the cosmos.

Chapter 6 begins with the question of secularity and explores whether or not the world is opposed to God. In this chapter I seek to examine the place of secularity in relation to evolution. For Teilhard, evolution *is* secular, and only one who can contemplate the world in its divine grandeur can see the world as a divine milieu. Teilhard's contribution to the question of secularity is profound, and his persistent plea that Christians see evolution as the very unfolding of God incarnate rendered a whole new understanding of Christian life that was influential on the spirit of Vatican II. His insecularization of God and the new emphasis of God involved in the history of an evolving cosmos are correctives we need in our own time to restore Christian life to its dynamic participation in the evolution of Christ within history.

I wrote *The Emergent Christ* because Christian life today is wearing thin. Some see the resurgence in traditional religious life, the renewal of the Tridentine mass, and the return of Latin as the best of times: finally, true Catholicism is being restored. Others see these as medieval remnants of a dying church, a church out of touch with a rapidly changing world. But catholicism is not an abstract universal concept; rather, it is a way of being religious in the world. To be catholic is to be engaged in evolution, a dynamic presence of relatedness with God that leads to greater wholes, to unity, to an evolution of consciousness that by its very nature enables God to be born from within. Chapter 7 takes up the question, Can the church evolve? Is it possible for the church to take evolution seriously, not as abstract theory but as the way God is at work in the world? Teilhard saw Christianity as a religion of evolution and envisioned a new phylum, a new evolutionary leap in cosmic life through the church and Christian life. Was this pure fantasy, as some may suggest? I do not think so. To be in Christ is to be in evolution, and unless we engage our lives as such, we fail both Christ and evolution, thwarting the inner evolutionary dynamic toward unity, justice, and peace. Christian life today is enervated by routinization, mediocrity, and internal divisions; the power to transform this world *so true* through love is corrupted by the power to dominate and control. Teilhard looked into the heart of the church and saw the immense power of love, which can unite and transform. In his view the church not only has the capacity to evolve, but evolution is its very nature precisely *because of*—and *not in spite of*—Jesus Christ. However, the church has not embraced evolution, nor does evolution affect Christian life. Hence, the church continues to function as a medieval construct, marginal to a global, complex world. *sad*

If Christian life is not only to survive but flourish, it needs rebirth. In Chapter 8 I discuss the inner universe, the evolution of the heart for evolution of the cosmos. We need a new interiority, a contemplation of the mystery of our lives that can lead to new freedom in love and new ways of living Christ in evolution. There can be no real evolution of Christ without an inner evolution in love. Chapter 9 brings together catholicity, Christ in evolution, and the institutional church to indicate something new that is emerging in our midst. There is a new appearance of Christ that is not of institutional religion but beyond it. It is a new *catholic* presence of openness and relatedness without explicit identification of being catholic. While the old *catholic* belongs to an institution burdened with divisions and internal conflicts, the new *catholic* is the breath of the Creator Spirit flowing in human hearts, the same way the Spirit flowed in the life of Jesus of Nazareth.

Yet, I am also convinced that Catholic Christians have a particular role in evolution. Participation in evolution is not an option for the baptized faithful; it is essential to the core of our faith in Jesus Christ. To evolve is to live in openness to the Creator Spirit, who continues to do new things in our midst. Evolution is the new wine of our time and must be poured into new wineskins. The old is not bad; it simply cannot contain the new wine. I discuss the creativity of the Spirit in view of systems and ask, Does Catholicism live as a closed system or an open system? Evolution requires openness to new influences and to new ways of giving birth to Christ.

Conversion is key to Catholic life in the twenty-first century because conversion is turning in grace toward new life—to participate in whole making and the emergence of Christ.

In light of evolution and quantum physics, Are these the best of times or the worst of times? may not be the best question to ask. Life is not a dichotomy of choices but a richness of possibilities. Quantum physics tells us the present moment is all we have; it is the power of now, as Eckhart Tolle reminds us.[15] We can help heal this world and unify it in love, or we can destroy its inner unity by our resistance to evolve in love. The problem of the emergence of Christ in evolution is not God's problem; rather, it is our fear of evolution and of God in evolution. We fear that a changing God is a fickle God, and a fickle God cannot be trusted. We have yet to grasp the reality that God is love, and love is dynamic; the fidelity of God's love lies in love's nature to change, grow, admonish, and yield. Love always seeks the best for the beloved. Until we grow into *this* God, who is love, a divine love that draws us from the future into the fullness of life, we can never accept the incarnation as the very purpose and goal of *this* creation. However, God is a beggar of love who waits at the soul's door without daring to force it open; God does not violate our freedom to create ourselves because divine love has imparted to us the freedom to be. The question of whether or not Christ will emerge as the ultimate personal center of this evolutionary universe is not a question of yes or no but a question of *how* Christ will evolve. God is love, and where there is love there is already the fullness of promise. Every moment is eternity in time. What do *we* want as members of the human species and as Christians? Do we want a world of unity, peace, and justice, or do we want another world, a world of heaven or artificial intelligence or a constructed world of religious life? Do we reject this world as gift, or do we simply resist our relatedness? Do we want to evolve, or to dissolve into history?

We are in a new axial age, and how we respond to the demands of our age is crucial.[16] We can evolve toward a healthy trans-humanism marked by the emergence of Christ—greater wholeness in our relationships to one another and to the earth—or we can shrink in fear that we will lose our identity and be overpowered by something outside our control. I am increasingly convinced that the root problem of our resistance to evolve lies in our resistance to change and thus a resistance to accept our inherent relatedness. Behind this resistance is the inability to accept the plurality of the triune God. Karl Rahner once remarked that "one could dispense with the doctrine of the Trinity as false and the major part of religious literature could well remain unchanged."[17] For all practical purposes, we are monists. Without the plurality of God we cannot grasp the emergence of Christ in evolution. Christ is not an individual but the personal center of plurality in unity. Where there is Christ there is complementarity of opposites and thus unity in love; hence, where there is Christ, there is peace. Evolution toward unity in love is evolution toward peace. It requires a growth in consciousness, a new awareness that the God of evolution is in evolution; the Omega is the evolver. Evolution continues despite our protests—or maybe because of them—because God is the evolver, and God desires to be born anew.

Chapter One

The Book of Creation

THE NEW COSMOS STORY

Patristic and medieval theologians, from Saint Augustine to Saint Bonaventure, were avid observers of the cosmos. Creation, Bonaventure wrote, is like a book from which we can gather insights about the Creator. The natural world bears the footprints of God, and the human person is created to read this book and know God. The school at Chartres in the twelfth century revived the cosmic Platonism of early writers and described a natural theology in which creation and Creator, divine and human, microcosm and macrocosm worked together for the perfection of the whole. Bonaventure claimed that the book of creation was the first book for humans to know God. However, sin rendered this book unintelligible, like a book written in a foreign language. The Word through whom all things are made (Jn 1) became flesh so that we could read the book of creation correctly as the book of God. Jesus, Bonaventure said, is the book written within and without.

It is important to return to the book of creation as the book of God because creation expresses God. Creation is not a backdrop for human drama but the disclosure of God's identity. The new book of creation today begins with two significant findings of modern science: evolution and quantum physics. The advent of evolutionary theory articulated by Charles Darwin and the upset of certainty in the physical universe initiated by Einstein's theories of relativity wrought cosmic upheaval on the levels of science, history, and culture at the beginning of the twentieth century. What was seen as a static, secure, stable, and unchanging universe was now seen to be dynamic, changing, novel, and creative. Supporting both pillars of the new science is the fundamental insight that the universe is in a process of coming to be.

The nice, neat universe of perfect order, running according to the Newtonian laws of motion, was destroyed in 1905 when Albert Einstein published a paper that upset the world of physics. For three hundred years Newton's vision of time and space as absolute was the sacred dogma of scientific cosmology. Space, for Newton, was an empty stage on which the drama of physics was played out, a constant emptiness everywhere and at all times. Time too was constant. No matter where one stood in the universe, time flowed at the same rate. Einstein's short, revolutionary paper swept away in a single stroke absolute space and time. Space is not an empty stage, nor does time flow at a fixed rate. Rather, space and time form a single dimension, each relative to the other. "Space and time could shrink or expand depending on the relative motion of the observers who measured them."[1] According to Adam Frank, "The new universe was a *hyperspace*, a world with an extra dimension. . . . In relativity every object becomes four-dimensional as it extends through time." Einstein's creative insight eventually yielded to a new understanding of gravity, which, for Newton, Frank says, was "the force between massive objects that pulled them toward each other."[2] The elastic nature of space-time impelled Einstein to think of gravity not as a substance but as a curvature of space-time by matter. It not only stretches or shrinks distances (depending on their direction with respect to the gravitational field) but also appears to slow down or "dilate" the flow of time. In other words, gravity acts to structure space, which is the basic ingredient of the universe.

Einstein's equations led to a most startling conclusion, which the great physicist-mathematician had to grapple with, that is, that the elastic nature of the universe implies change. Einstein himself was not comfortable with this insight. In 1916 Dutch physicist Willem de Sitter constructed a universe that could stretch in different directions, "like taffy," a theoretical insight that received experimental support in 1928 when astronomer Edwin Hubble, "using the most powerful telescope of his day, found that every galaxy in the sky was moving away from us."[3] He saw that ours was not the only galaxy; there were many galaxies with large empty spaces between them. "The more distant a galaxy was from our own, the faster it appeared to be rushing outward."[4] If the universe was contracting instead of expanding, we would see distant galaxies radiate a blue light intensity (measured by the Doppler effect) proportional to their distance. However, Hubble noticed a red shift, indicating that the distance between galaxies is expanding. "This is exactly what observers riding on debris from an explosion would see. In an explosive release of matter all the bits of shrapnel appear to move away from all the others."[5]

The idea that the universe is dynamic and changing was confirmed in 1964 when two scientists working at Bell Laboratories in New Jersey discovered "cosmic microwave background" that was left over from the beginning of the universe, more than thirteen billion years ago. Adam Frank writes:

> New Jersey seems an unlikely place for the origin of the universe to reveal itself, but that is exactly where the story of the Big Bang starts. . . . At the time the two astronomers were working on the new technology of microwave communications. . . . The problem was an annoying, low level of "noise" that persisted regardless of which direction the antenna pointed. It was a microwave hiss that refused to go away. . . . The microwave signal that Arno Penzias captured wasn't noise but the ultimate prehistoric relic. . . . It was a pervasive electromagnetic memory of the universe's origin and a direct link to the time of the Big Bang.[6]

Up to the time of the discovery by Arno Penzias, scientists believed that the cosmos had an eternal, steady state. British scientist Fred Hoyle suggested that even as galaxies moved away and the universe expanded, matter was slowly added to the universe. Hoyle did not accept the Big Bang theory of the universe proposed by the Belgium priest George LeMaitre because it smacked too easily of a Creator God. Hoyle's steady-state model, however, was not convincing against the discovery of the cosmic microwave background. Rather the elastic space-time universe glowing with the relics of a primeval explosion supported the idea that the universe had a beginning, a Big Bang; the universe developed from an extremely dense and hot state.

Einstein's revolutionary ideas sparked a new vision of the cosmos, a new genesis story. It is such an incredible story that I must let the astronomer Adam Frank describe it in his own words:

In the beginning there was a single geometrical point containing all space, time, matter and energy. This point did not sit in space. It was space. There was no inside and no outside. Then "it" happened. The point "exploded" and the Universe began to expand. . . . The universe had a temperature of 100 billion degrees at this point and was so dense that a single teaspoon of cosmic matter would weigh more than a thousand tons. . . . At one one-hundredth of a second after the Big Bang the entire universe was about the size of our solar system. It was a universe pervaded by dense, primordial gas: an ultra-smooth, ultra-hot sea of protons, neutrons, and other subatomic particles. . . . In this dense soup, photons, which are quantum particles of light, mixed easily with matter. . . . As the cosmic clock ticked off the instants, expansion continued to stretch space, and with it the particle-photon sea thinned and cooled. . . . Protons and neutrons collided and combined to form nuclei of light elements such as helium and lithium. . . . This cosmic nuclear furnace stopped just three minutes after the Big Bang when the universe dropped below the temperatures and densities at which nuclear reactions can be sustained. At this point all creation was a mix of photons, protons, electrons, and light nuclei. . . . After 300,000 years of expansion and cooling, negatively charged electrons were moving slowly enough to get caught by positively charged protons. Each capture created a new atom of hydrogen. Once the process started, the universe rapidly made the transition from a mix of free photons and electrons to a vast gas of electronically neutral atomic hydrogen. . . . As the eons passed a vast cosmic network of form emerged from these humble beginnings. One by one a hierarchy of cosmic shapes was born. Galaxies appeared first. Then clusters of galaxies were swept together by their mutual gravitational pull. . . . Gravity alone constructed a cosmic architecture that is filamentary and beautiful. . . . [But] the universe is also composed of tremendous

quantities of something else, something that emits no light.
. . . This "dark matter" constitutes the majority of mass in
the universe. . . . It is dark matter . . . that sculpts the large-
scale structure. . . . The visible galaxies we see strewn across
space are nothing more than strings of luminous flotsam
drifting on an invisible sea of dark matter.[7]

Today we know our universe to be ancient, large, dynamic, and
interconnected. The universe is about 13.7 billion years old, with a
future of billions of years before it. Some scientists estimate that
the universe will exist for 100 trillion years, although the sun will
die out long before then. It is a large universe, stretching light
years in diameter, one of billions of galaxies in the observable
universe. Our own galaxy, the Milky Way, is one among billions
of galaxies in the observable universe, consisting of 100 billion
stars, and stretching about 100,000 light years in diameter. The
galaxies are often grouped into clusters—some clusters having as
many as two thousand galaxies. What is amazing about this story
is that we are here to tell it. The universe is finely tuned for carbon-based life, at least on planet earth. While some scientists say
that we are here because this is the only universe (out of an infinite number) in which conditions were just right for the emergence of humans (strong anthropic principle), others claim that
in a universe large or infinite in space-time, the conditions necessary for life will be met only in certain regions that are limited in
space and time (weak anthropic principle).[8] However we understand this amazingly fine-tuned universe, the embodied persons
that we are at this very moment—all the constituents that have
come together to form our own physical being—were present in
the Big Bang, at the beginning of this universe. "A trillionth of a
trillionth of a trillionth of one percent faster, the cosmic material
would have been flung too far apart for anything significant to
happen."[9] We would not be here today to tell the story. But the
fact is, we humans are the universe come to consciousness. This
is a radically different universe from the one Ptolemy described:
static, hierarchical, orderly, concentric. This new cosmic story is
thoroughly dynamic, and if we are to have a credible theology of
God in this universe, it must begin with this dynamic story of the
universe.

THE EVOLUTION OF HUMANS

Charles Darwin did for biology what Albert Einstein did for physics: rent asunder the established understanding of nature. The theory of evolution that emerged among nineteenth-century biologists such as Alfred Wallace was made famous by Charles Darwin in his *Origin of the Species by Means of Natural Selection*. What Darwin sought to show was that natural life unfolds primarily through the process of natural selection, "a process that promotes or maintains adaptation and, thus, gives the appearance of purpose or design."[10] Although he used the word *evolve* only once in that work (in the very last sentence) his name became synonymous with evolution. Darwin's denial of design in nature was almost universally interpreted as a denial of the divine in nature.[11] For those who believe in God, Darwin's offense lay in the proposal that natural selection is a blind, purposeful process that operates through random variations, and that this aimless mechanism accounts for all forms of life on earth. American philosopher Daniel Dennett called Darwin's theory of evolution by natural selection a "dangerous idea" because it challenges religious belief that the universe is here for a reason.[12] Does evolution displace religion, or is it a "gift to theology," as John Haught argues? Evolutionary science compels theology to reclaim features of religious faith that are all too easily smothered by the deadening disguise of order and design.[13] Haught writes that "Darwin dropped a religiously explosive bomb into the Victorian culture of his contemporaries, and Christians ever since, including some but not all theologians, have been scrambling to defuse it or toss it out of harm's way."[14]

The epic of evolution may be the greatest story ever told because it speaks of the world's struggle toward an expansive freedom in the presence of self-giving grace.[15] What Darwin showed is that change in the biological world is not due to outside forces or purposeful function of an organism but to aspects within nature itself, especially the natural selection of traits for adaptation to the environment.[16] The science of genetics today helps us realize that a genetic mutation can lead to new characteristics in an organism, just as a natural disaster can change the environment to which an organism must adapt. Life is malleable, and the interlocking constellation of

relationships is what forms any one being. Evolution helps us realize that God works through the messiness of creation and is less
concerned with imposing design on processes than providing nature with opportunities to participate in its own creation.

The modern theory of evolution (the neo-Darwinian synthesis)
says that the great diversity of life can be *naturally* explained by the
combination of chance, law, and deep time. *Chance* means that life
is not predetermined or planned; rather, it is loaded with random
events or contingencies. While chance is integral to nature, it works
together with laws within nature. For example, the law of natural
selection "selects" as survivors organisms that best adapt to the
environment, transmitting their genetic characteristics to succeed-
ing generations, while all others perish. Most of all, evolution requires enormous time. Human beings appear after billions of years
of cataclysmic events and mass extinctions. John Haught offers a
helpful image to show the time that evolution requires. Imagine,
he says, the encyclopedia of life in thirty volumes. Each volume has
450 pages, and each page is equal to one million years. Volume 1 is
the Big Bang; volume 21 is the earth; volume 29 is the Cambrian
period; mammals appear in volume 30, the final volume, on page
390. On the last page of this last volume, the last two words are
Homo sapiens![17]

The story of humans within evolutionary history began ago when
the earth and other planets started forming around the young sun.
Over this long period of time, life evolved from enucleated bacte-
rial cells to nucleated cells, which could eventually replicate into
multi-cellular animals. Humans, like mammals, have existed on earth
for a relatively short time, only about 0.04 percent of the earth's 4.5
years of existence. The modern human physique first appeared in
Africa about 150,000 years ago, and then spread into the rest of the
Old World, replacing existing populations of human forms.[18] William Grassie indicates that humans and our most immediate homi-
nid ancestors evolved as hunters and gatherers in small tribes and
extended families:

> Humans existed as small hunter-gather tribes for over 50,000
> generations before the advent of agriculture. Our ancestors
> adapted and lived successfully in diverse climates starting in
> the savannas of Africa and then traveling to coastal regions,

tropical rain forests, high mountains, and cold arctic regions. Our ancestors survived a major global climatic catastrophe some 70,000 years ago with the explosion of Mount Toba in Sumatra. This super-volcanic eruption, estimated to be three thousand times greater than the 1980 eruption of Mount Saint Helens, changed everything overnight. The volcanic ash released in the atmosphere reduced average global temperature by 5 degrees Celsius for seven years and triggered a global ice age. Sri Lanka, India, and Pakistan were covered with 5 meters of volcanic ash. Humanity was reduced to some 1,000 to 10,000 breeding pairs. And yet we survived, and as the sky cleared and the ice slowly retreated over the millennia, we resumed our expansion, eventually migrating to every continent except Antarctica.[19]

The whole history of the universe, and particularly the history of biological life on earth, has been characterized by the steady emergence of complexity, a movement toward more complex life forms, which, at critical points in the evolutionary process, qualitative differences emerge. The term *evolution* can be extended beyond its biological meaning and applied to the whole cosmic process. This progressive evolutionary movement, according to Teilhard, is one in which the consistence of the elements and their stability of balance lie in the direction not of matter but of spirit.[20] This movement from matter to spirit, in Teilhard's view, marks "the fundamental property of the cosmic mass to concentrate upon itself . . . as a result of attraction of synthesis."[21] Biological evolution begins on the level of physical convergence or joining of disparate elements to form new entities; life prefers increased life.

The term *emergence* is used today to describe the appearance of novelty in nature. Emergence is irreducible novelty of increasing complexity, a combination of holism with novelty in a way that contrasts with both physical reductionism and dualism. Philip Clayton defines emergence as "genuinely new properties which are not reducible to what came before, although they are continuous with it."[22] He writes: "Once there was no universe and then, after the Big Bang, there was an exploding world of stars and galaxies. Once the earth was unpopulated and later it was teeming with primitive life forms. Once there were apes living in trees and then there were Mozart, Einstein and Gandhi."[23] From galaxies to Gandhi, emergence may be a way the Big Bang repeats itself as the universe continues to unfold. At some point evolution reaches a reflexive state that generates the idea of evolution, the point of Homo sapiens—we know that we know. We are evolution become conscious of itself.[24]

THE GIFT OF EVOLUTION

Teilhard de Chardin believed that evolution is the way God is present to creation and said that Christians should love evolution because of its God-centeredness.[25] Evolution, however, is less loved than feared. It sends shudders down many people's spines because it seems to reduce the human person to a monkey and defies our image of God's power to create. In an excellent book entitled *Responses to 101 Questions on God and Evolution,* John Haught provides a clear and thorough explanation of evolution that seeks to clarify the relationship between evolution and Christianity and dispel the fears of anti-evolutionists.[26] I can only recapitulate briefly what Haught articulates in his many books, namely, there is no inherent conflict between evolution and Christian doctrine. On the contrary, evolution has liberated Christian doctrine from the grip of Greek metaphysics and has renewed the God of biblical promise. To appreciate Haught's insights, it is important to know the basic history of Christian theology and the science of evolution, which he offers in his works. As he and others point out, evolution is not a theory to believe in; it is not a religion. Rather, it is an understanding of how mechanisms within nature promote species diversity and development and, on the cosmic level, how the universe progresses from the Big Bang to human life.

Darwin's theory of evolution, according to Haught, is remarkably simple. It has two main facets: "First all forms of life descend by way of gradual modification over the course of time from a common ancestor; and second, the explanation of this gradual modification, including the emergence of new species, is *natural selection.* Natural selection means that those organisms most able to adapt to their environments will be 'selected' by nature to survive and produce offspring, while nonadaptive organisms will perish."[27] Today, developments in genetics and molecular biology have greatly enriched Darwin's theory of evolution and provide great insight into the emergence and development of new species and, indeed, new cosmic life.

Despite the remarkable achievements in research science in the twentieth century, the majority of Americans do not know much about the science of evolution, nor do they know the difference between evolution, intelligent design and creationism. According to Michael Specter, "The results of a California Academy of Sciences poll in 2009 revealed that only fifty three percent of American adults know how long it takes for the Earth to revolve around the sun, and a slightly larger number—fifty nine percent—are aware that dinosaurs and humans never lived at the same time."[28] According to a 2009 Gallup poll only 39 percent of Americans accept the theory of evolution; of these, 74 percent have postgraduate degrees, while 21 percent ended their education with high school. Even more telling is that 55 percent of those who accept evolution do not attend church; only 24 percent of weekly churchgoers accept it.[29] Evolution and religion continue to be in conflict, less among Catholic Christians than among Protestant evangelical Christians.

The Catholic Church has taken a more flexible approach to evolution because of a less literal interpretation of Genesis than some Protestant denominations. Pope Pius XII, a deeply conservative man, directly addressed the issue of evolution in a 1950 encyclical *Humani Generis*. The document reveals the pope's hope that evolution will be a passing scientific fad and attacks those persons who "imprudently and indiscreetly hold that evolution . . . explains the origin of all things" (no. 5). Nonetheless, Pius XII states that nothing in Catholic doctrine is contradicted by a theory that suggests one species might evolve into another—even if that species is Homo sapiens:

> The Teaching Authority of the Church does not forbid that, in conformity with the present state of human sciences and sacred theology, research and discussions, on the part of men experienced in both fields, take place with regard to the doctrine of evolution, in as far as it inquires into the origin of the human body as coming from pre-existent and living matter— for the Catholic faith obliges us to hold that souls are immediately created by God. (no. 36)

Pius XII cautioned that evolution is still a theory and should not be accepted as though it were a certain proven doctrine. Pope John Paul II revisited the question of evolution in a message to the Pontifical Academy of Sciences in 1996. The pontiff began his statement with the hope that "we will be able to profit from the fruitfulness of a trustful dialogue between the Church and science."[30] He recognized that science and scripture sometimes have "apparent contradictions," but said that when this is the case, a "solution" must be found because "truth cannot contradict truth." On the scientific merits of evolution, John Paul said, "Today, almost half a century after publication of the encyclical, new knowledge has led to the recognition of the theory of evolution as more than a hypothesis."[31]

While John Paul's statement on evolution was received favorably by the scientific community, creationists expressed dismay at the pontiff's words and suggested that the initial news reports might have been based on a faulty translation, especially since John Paul gave the speech in French.[32] However, the pope clearly accepted evolution as an explanation for the development of life, without specifying the mechanisms of evolution that belong to science. In a 2008 conference sponsored by the Vatican on the occasion of the 150th anniversary of the publication of Charles Darwin's *The Origin of Species*, Archbishop Gianfranco Ravasi, president of the Pontifical Council for Culture, affirmed that evolutionary theory is "not incompatible" with the teachings of the Catholic Church, with the message of the Bible, and with theology, indicating that the Vatican remains open to evolution as an explanation for the development of life without identifying any particular mechanisms of evolution.[33] It is interesting that this conference on evolution sponsored by the Vatican did not include supporters of creationism and intelligent design. Organizers of the conference indicated their desire to foster a dialogue that was strictly scientific, discussing rational philosophy and theology along with the latest scientific discoveries. According to Jesuit Father Marc Leclerc, intelligent design "substitutes divine will for the mechanism which is the province of science to study, even though this is obviously a matter of two distinct levels [of causation]."[34] Despite the Vatican's support of evolution, a growing number of Catholics believe that evolution is incompatible with Catholic doctrine because it suggests a world without God, a world in which randomness and chance are the ultimate realities. Some opt instead for intelligent design which promotes a designer at work in creation. Yet, at the most fundamental level, Christianity is wholly compatible with evolution.

THE STRANGE QUANTUM WORLD

While astronomers and physicists have been mapping the large-scale universe, other scientists have been exploring the world of quantum physics. One of the discoverers of quantum physics, the Danish physicist Niels Bohr, remarked, "If you are not confused or shocked by quantum physics, then you have not really understood it."[35] Quantum physics teaches that what we think of as matter is actually the manifestation of energy, what physicists call quanta or little packets or lumps of energy manifesting themselves out of an infinite field. The realization that light, which had been primarily understood to be waves, actually exhibited properties we call photons, little quanta of energy, led physicists to ask, If light can behave like particles, can particles behave like waves? This question led scientists to do the double-slit experiment with electrons.[36] In this experiment a background board with two slits is set up. As a particle goes through one slit or another, its wavefunction goes through both slits and suffers interference. Since the wavefunction guides the particle's motion, it is impossible to measure the wavefunction without affecting the particle's position. Because "there is no separate stage of wavefunction collapse, if you measure a particle's position and find it *here* that is truly where it was a moment before the measurement took place."[37] Scientists found that light has a dual nature; in some cases it behaves as a wave, and in other cases it behaves as a photon. So which is it? When it looks like a particle, it *is* a particle. When it looks like a wave, it *is* a wave. *It is meaningless to ascribe any properties or even existence to anything that has not been measured.* What quantum physics tells us is that *nothing is real unless it is observed*; it is a participatory universe. John Gribbin writes, "When we try to look at the spread-out electron wave, it collapses into a definite particle, but when we are not looking it keeps its options open. . . . Unless someone looks, nature herself does not know which hole the electron is going through."[38]

Niels Bohr called this wave/particle aspect of reality complementarity, which means "neither description is complete in itself, but there are circumstances when it is more appropriate to use the particle concept and circumstances where it is better to use the wave concept."[39] German physicist Werner Heisenberg indicated that uncertainty is part of dynamic nature of particles, since the more precisely the position of a particle is determined, the less precisely the momentum is known. We do not live in a deterministic universe; hence, what cannot be measured cannot take place exactly. It is a participatory universe with no distinction between the process of observation and what is observed; that is, there is no line between subject and object. Only what can be observed can be known. Thus we are actors rather than spectators in the universe.

While physicists struggled with the discovery of relativity and the mysterious nature of matter and energy, biologists began looking at living systems as integrated wholes. Just as in quantum physics there are no "parts," in biology a "part" became identified as a "pattern in an inseparable web of relationships."[40] This insight led scientists to conclude that matter is not composed of basic building blocks but rather of complicated webs of relations in which the observer constitutes a final link in the chain of observational processes, and the properties of any atomic object can be understood only in terms of interaction between object and observer. Ludwig von Bertalanffy, who is credited with the development of *systems thinking* as a major scientific movement, began his career as a biologist in Vienna in the 1920s and soon after joined the Vienna Circle of scientists and philosophers. In light of evolution Bertalanffy strove to replace the mechanistic foundations of science with a holistic vision based on systems thinking. He wrote: "Whereas Newtonian mechanics was a science of forces and trajectories, evolutionary thinking—thinking in terms of change, growth and development, required a new science of complexity."[41]

A system is commonly defined as a group of interacting units or elements that have a common purpose. Open systems refer to systems that interact with other systems or the outside environment, whereas closed systems refer to systems having relatively little interaction with other systems or the outside environment.[42] Systems that are open arise from interactions and relationships among parts. The properties of parts can be understood only from organization of whole; hence the key to an open system is not the individual units of the system but the principles of organization. Living organisms are considered open systems because they take in substances from their environment such as food and air and return other substances to their environment. For example, humans inhale oxygen out of the environment and exhale carbon dioxide into the environment. In contrast, a closed system is a relatively self-contained, self-maintaining unit that has little interaction or exchange with its environment.

According to Bertalanffy, living organisms are open systems that cannot be described by classical thermodynamics because, in classical systems, there is an irretrievable drive toward entropy and heat. Open systems, he indicated, feed on a continual flux of matter and energy from their environment to stay alive. Fritjof Capra writes: "Unlike closed systems which settle into a state of thermal equilibrium, open systems maintain themselves far from equilibrium in this 'steady state' (of openness) characterized by continual flow and change."[43]

In the early 1960s meteorologist Edward Lorenz was studying weather patterns using computer simulations and found that open systems are sensitive to initial conditions and can produce complex and unpredictable results over time. Frustrated with the slow computational process of the computer, he went off for a long coffee break and returned to his office to find something startling on his screen: an entirely new pattern from that predicted. Lorenz discovered that small changes in initial conditions can produce large changes in the long-term outcome. This discovery became known as chaos theory, not because of its randomness but because underlying order exists in apparently random data. Chaos theory has three main points: (1) *sensitivity to initial conditions*, which means arbitrarily small perturbations of the current trajectory may lead to significantly different future behaviors (the term *butterfly effect* was coined to describe this phenomenon); (2) *strange attractors*, which means basins of attraction within a system can lure the system into new patterns of order over time; and (3) *fractals*, which are the geometric shapes formed from repeated patterns of behavior at different scales.[44]

Chaos theory forms an integral part of systems thinking. The physical world is relational; systems form out of interacting relationships. Far different from the medieval construct of the Great

Chain of Being, being itself seems to concentrate not on building blocks but on principles of organization. The world appears as a complicated tissue of events in which connections of different kinds alternate or overlap or combine, determining the texture of the whole. In this respect causality requires a whole new understanding, because thinking is no longer analytically linear but integral and contextual. Everything in the universe is "genetically" related. The universe is bound together in communion, each thing with all the rest. Physicist Brian Swimme states, "The universe shivers with wonder in the depths of the human."[45] We live in interwoven layers of bondedness. The world is not a "machine" but an integrated whole, which means the network of phenomena that compose the stuff of life is fundamentally interconnected and interdependent. In *this* world we humans do not occupy the center of the universe; neither are we superior to all other living beings. Rather, the interconnectedness of life in our universe means that we are part of a web of life. Integral systems tell us that our universe is thoroughly interconnected, so that even our own being is not *our own*. Reality by its very nature is interconnected.

UNDIVIDED WHOLENESS

We are coming to a new understanding of reality or, what philosophy has grappled with for ages, a new understanding of being. Relationship is not a *quality* of being, as Aristotle thought; it *is* being. To be is to be related. Although theology has built a whole system of metaphysics based on Aristotle's notion of being, such a system holds little weight in the face of modern physics. Quantum physics has fundamentally changed our understanding of being. Words like *matter, form,* and *being* are neither substantive nor conceptual. Rather, they point to a whole new understanding of reality that is radically different from the worlds of Augustine, Thomas, and Bonaventure. It is not a stretch to say that the whole theological enterprise must be rebuilt from the bottom up.

Albert Einstein had problems with quantum physics, especially with the uncertain nature of events and the strange interaction among particles. In 1935 Einstein and his postdoctoral research associates Boris Podolsky and Nathan Rosen performed a thought experiment based on insights from quantum physics to see if indeed particles could affect one another at a distance without interacting. Generally referred to as EPR, their work quickly became a centerpiece in the debate over the interpretation of the quantum theory, a debate that continues today.[46] The experiment focused on a quantum particle split in half, with the halves heading off in opposite directions. The scientists posited one half of the particle spinning in one direction and the other half spinning in the opposite direction. The total spin, they conjectured, must be zero by the conversation of the spin at the point at which the parent split. If the particles are separated by distance, measurement of particle A as "up" will influence the measurement of particle B as "down." The measurement on A does not merely reveal an already established state of B: it actually *produces* that state which renders the particles entangled. The object of the experiment was to show that measurements performed on spatially separated parts of a quantum system can apparently have an instantaneous influence on one another. This effect is now known as *nonlocal behavior* (or *quantum weirdness* or *spooky action at a distance*). Physicist Erwin Schrödinger said: "If two separated bodies, each by itself known maximally, enter a situation in which they influence each other, and separate again, then there occurs regularly that which I have just called *entanglement* of our knowledge of the two bodies."[47] Quantum entanglement is nonlocal interaction or unmediated action at a distance; that is, a nonlocal interaction can link up one location with another without crossing space, without decay, and without delay.[48]

Einstein's original intention in performing the EPR experiment was to show the difficulty with quantum theory. The idea of nonlocal action at a distance requires a connection that travels faster than light, an idea that conflicted with Einstein's relativity theory. However David Bohm and his colleagues did not see the EPR experiment as showing a problem with quantum physics. Rather, they interpreted the nonlocal effects as pointing to something new in reality that could not be attributed to causal connections. In 1982 Alain Aspect and his team performed the actual experiment that verified nonlocal action at a distance as an important aspect of quantum physics. Bohm attributed the strange phenomenon of nonlocality to hidden variables; moreover, he developed the idea of *holomovement* or *implicate order* as his primary explanation.[49]

Rather than starting with the parts and explaining the whole in terms of the parts, Bohm started with a notion of undivided wholeness and derived the parts as abstractions from the whole. He called this unbroken order "implicate order," indicating an enfolding of events. Implicate order is a way of looking at reality not merely in terms of external interactions among things, but in terms of the internal (enfolded) relationships among things. As human beings and societies we seem separate, but in our roots we are part of an indivisible whole and share in the same cosmic process. The term *holomovement* describes the unbroken and undivided totality of implicate order. Movement is primary; what seem like permanent structures are only relatively autonomous sub-entities that emerge out of the whole of flowing movement and then dissolve back into an unceasing process of becoming. Each relatively autonomous and stable structure is to be understood as a product that has been formed in the whole flowing movement and that will ultimately dissolve back into this movement, not as something independently and permanently existent. How it forms and maintains itself depends on its place or function within the whole.[50]

Bohm's theory of implicate order is based on several important ideas. First, being is intrinsically relational and exists as unbroken wholeness in a system. Whereas classical physics is based on parts making up wholes, Bohm took relationships among parts as primary. Each part is connected with every other part at the quantum level. Thus, the whole universe is the basic reality; primacy belongs to the whole. Because reality exists in systems, every system is a supersystem; systems exist within systems. Second, systems are in movement, or holomovement, and process reality is a dynamic creation. As Kevin Sharpe explains: "The holomovement model for reality comes from the properties of a holographic image of an object. . . . Any portion of the holographic plate (the hologram) contains information on the whole object."[51] Third, because reality is marked by relationality and movement, it has endless depth. What we know of reality does not exhaust it; properties and qualities will always be beyond us. Hence, Bohm directs us to think in wholes, relationality, and depth, insights that led to the description of the holon, something that is simultaneously a whole and a part.[52]

Arthur Koestler proposed the word *holon* to describe the hybrid nature of sub-wholes and parts within *in vivo* systems. From this perspective, holons exist simultaneously as self-contained wholes in relation to their subordinate parts, and dependent parts when considered from the inverse direction. Koestler defines *holarchy* as a hierarchy of self-regulating holons. These holons function, first, as autonomous wholes in supra-ordination to their parts; second, as dependent parts in subordination to controls on higher levels; and third, in coordination with their local environment. The number of levels in a holarchy describes its depth.[53] Ken Wilber notes that evolution produces greater depth and less span, that is, as the individual holon acquires greater depth, the span or the collective gets smaller and smaller.[54] For example, a whole atom is part of a whole molecule; a whole molecule is part of a whole cell; a whole cell is part of a whole organism. Similarly, we can see human persons as individual and yet as a part within a whole community, which is, in turn, a part within a whole society. Reality is composed of neither wholes nor parts but of whole/parts, or holons, which Ken Wilber calls integral systems.[55] The physical universe is thoroughly interrelated, and we are integral holons of the evolving web.

Bohm's implicate order or unbroken wholeness in movement has influenced British biologist Rupert Sheldrake, who describes an organic model of biological behavior over a mechanistic one. Sheldrake postulated that repetitive behavior creates informational fields that can influence similar behavior in an unrelated area. He calls these informational fields "morphogenetic" fields because they are formative fields (*morphe*, or "form") that carry information, not energy, and are available throughout time and space without any loss of intensity after they have been created. Morphogenetic fields are unseen forces that preserve the *form* of self-organizing systems, maintaining order from within. That is, morphogenetic fields direct other members of the species toward the same form or behavior, or what Sheldrake calls "morphic resonance." According to Sheldrake, these fields of habitual patterns link all people. The more people have a habit or pattern—whether of knowledge, perception, or behavior—the stronger it is in the field, and the more easily it replicates in a new person (or entity).

Here is one example. "Sheldrake took three short, similar Japanese rhymes—one a meaningless jumble of disconnected Japanese words, the second a newly-composed verse and the third a traditional rhyme known by millions of Japanese." Neither he nor the English schoolchildren he had memorize these verses knew which was which, nor did they know any Japanese. "The most easily-learned rhyme turned out to be the one well-known to Japanese."[56] The discovery of morphogenetic fields can be used to describe how human consciousness is shared. A newly forming system "tunes into" a previous system by having within it a "seed" that resonates with a similar seed in the earlier form. As more and more people learn or do something, it becomes easier for others to learn or do it.[57] The question is, What creates the first form?; it is, after all, this form that creates the morphogenetic field. Sheldrake, like Bohm, postulates hidden variables or principles within systems that act creatively, perhaps something like strange attractors due to the open unpredictable behavior of systems. Or perhaps the material world is laden with potential forms that are realized under certain conditions over time.[58] The origin of morphogenetic fields remains unknown.

Although science continues to shed new light on evolution and quantum physics, it is clear that our understanding of matter and form has radically changed. Even the word *being* must be understood in a new way that includes relatedness, implicate order, plasticity (ability to change), and endless depth.[59] Our view of reality has been deconstructed from its medieval synthesis because it is no longer a static, objective view outside the observer. We can now say that reality is thoroughly interrelated and replete with mystery. Relationship, mystery, and evolution form the new trinity of reality that we call God.

Chapter Two

The Evolution of God

We are struggling today to make sense of God in this evolutionary universe, especially as physics continues to disclose a strange world of quantum events and evolution is speeding up through technology. We are straddling the old and the new. The new scientific paradigm is still not clear enough for an imprimatur, and yet it is significantly different from the world of Newton and certainly from the world of Aristotle. Despite this, many people are not familiar with the insights of modern science. Efforts are made to fit Thomas Aquinas's God into a post-Einsteinian universe, as if adjusting a few ideas will balance his medieval system in the postmodern period. However, it is like trying to fit a square peg into a round hole; it just doesn't work. One of the main questions today is the question of God. What does the name *God* mean in an evolutionary, quantum universe? Who is the God of evolution? Can we talk about God and creation as if there are two distinct types of being in the universe? Can we adequately speak of God's being and created being in a world of reality where *being* is another word for interrelatedness? The challenges facing theology today are immense, and it does not suffice to rearrange the parts of a medieval theological synthesis to suit the needs of a twenty-first century universe. "A mistake about creation will lead to a mistake about God," Thomas Aquinas remarked.[1] We need to know the book of creation today, as science informs us, to know God.

Although the new physics is still a fertile field for exploration, the radical shift from the world of classical mechanics is enough to warrant a new understanding of being and hence theology. David Bohm's idea of implicate order holds promise for a new understanding of

being, primarily because it upholds the primacy of order as a function of relationship. As we indicated in the last chapter, Bohm's
system builds on several fundamental ideas that include the constitutive relationality of the universe, the relationality of being, and
the endless depth of being, what he calls unified wholeness in constant movement. Bohm indicates that every particle is actually a
manifestation of the whole and that nothing can be understood
except within the context of the whole. When it comes to theology
we must ask: What is God in relation to the whole? If nothing can
be understood apart from interactions in the whole, how do we
understand God and creation? What if we were to view God and
creation not as two orders of being but simply as a conceptual order of being that is thoroughly interrelated? Could we think of
God as divine, uncreated implicate order of being, the endless depth,
movement, process, and relatedness of being? Created being then
would relate to uncreated being as explicit order relates to implicate order. We could conceive of God and creation as interrelated
divine and created energies. Could we then think of God not as
other to the world but as the inner dynamic of the world, that is,
the world within God? To see the world from within God is to see
the world in its wholeness, in its unity. In a study on Meister Eckhart,
Cyprian Smith writes:

> Instead of standing within the created world, looking in it for
> signs of a God who is outside it, we stand within God, and it
> is the world which now appears outside. When we stand within
> the world, God appears as totally transcendent and "other."
> When we stand within God, however, it is the world which
> appears as "other," but not by any means transcendent; on
> the contrary, we are greater than it. It appears as a pale and
> imperfect reflection of the dazzling and brilliant Truth in
> which we are living and making our home.[2]

Evolution is the gathering of being toward wholeness, to become
more unified in our "home" because this is the nature of being
itself. Every level of being—cosmic, personal, spiritual—is evolving toward wholeness. God is unbroken wholeness in movement,
and creation is movement toward God-centered wholeness.
Hence, we do not come from the whole and exist as disparate
parts longing for the whole, as Plato surmised. Rather, our very

being *is* the whole; to be related to God is to become whole within whole.

It seems the time is ripe to begin thinking of theology not in terms of parts but in terms of wholes: the whole person in the whole creation in the whole God. We are wholes within wholes, interrelated on every level. The nature of being is interrelated wholeness, and evolution is wholeness in movement toward greater wholeness. If the God-world relationship is wholeness in evolution, then God is in evolution. God is that which is thoroughly related, infinite in depth, and constant in movement. Quantum physics and evolution tell us that the God of the philosophers, the God of Abraham and Moses, the God revealed in the burning bush has been revealed anew in the Big Bang. This is not the God of the great chain of Being or the paternal figure of the medieval cosmos. This God is interrelated depth and movement. The creator God of an evolutionary, interrelated universe is an evolutionary, interrelated God. God is unbroken wholeness in movement; God is in evolution.

THE PROBLEM OF CHANGE

Evolution is based on change. When applied to biology, evolution generally refers to changes in life forms over time. The same concept of change over time can be applied to the cosmos. Life means change, and the rich diversity of life is based on change. One does not have to be trained in science to realize that change is integral to life. All of life follows the cycle of birth, maturity, deterioration, and death. Change is not only relevant to life but to all life's expressions in culture, education, politics, economics, and history. If evolution describes creation, and evolution means change, then change must be integral to God, who is Creator. By separating evolution from God, placing God over and against evolution, we separate creation from Creator and wind up with an irrelevant God and a self-sufficient materialism.

A number of years ago Fritjof Capra wrote *The Tao of Physics*, indicating that Buddhism shares similarities with quantum physics. According to Capra, the interrelated quantum universe runs by a bootstrap that is, in a sense, a metaphysics of the universe.[3] In this model the universe is a dynamic web of related events with no basic parts or properties, whether laws, equations, or principles. Any property or part of the universe follows from the properties of all the other parts. The harmony of all the relationships among the parts determines the structure of the entire web. Thus the universe pulls itself up by its own bootstrap. I think a similar comparison could be made between Christianity and evolution.

Teilhard de Chardin noted over fifty years ago that Christianity is a religion of evolution. The very claim that God *becomes* something other than God points to change within God. This may surprise us, but from a Christian perspective could God *become* a human person *without* change? Could the resurrection of Jesus Christ really bring about new creation *without* changing the relationship of human life to God? The problem of God "changing" arises when we consider God as unified and hence inert substance—the problem of being. However, scripture states that "God is love" (1 Jn 4:8), and love by its very nature is dynamic and relational. Love is energy and spirit. Change, therefore, cannot be extrinsic to God; rather, if God is love, then God is change.

Alfred North Whitehead took up the question of change in an evolutionary world and developed a new understanding of God in relation to a changing world. His process theology is based on the idea that change is integral to God, because God is love. For Whitehead, love defines both God's nature and activity. Classical theism has so stressed God's independence and absoluteness, his character as "un-moved mover," "first cause," or "ground of being," that love hardly seems to be God's essential quality or characteristic. Whitehead was insistent that the concrete actuality of God is found in concrete nature rather than in the more abstract aspects of the divine nature. Love cannot be known except in relationships, in being affected as well as affecting, in sharing and participating. God is the cosmic Lover who tenderly, luringly, persuasively, faithfully, indefatigably, inexhaustibly (for God's caring never comes to the end) relates to, cares for, and brings all possible good out of the world. Describing Whitehead's philosophy, Haught writes:

> God influences the cosmos by holding out before it new ways of becoming itself. . . . The world is in evolution because God is a God of *persuasive* rather than coercive power. . . . Evolution occurs because God is more interested in *adventure* than in preserving the status quo. . . . Process theology argues that

the God of biblical religion is a God of persuasive love, the source of novelty and the stimulus to adventure.[4]

Process, therefore, rather than substance should be taken as the fundamental metaphysical constituent of the world and hence of God's relation to the world. Process is, in a sense, moving forward or the moving forward of a particular order. God is in process because God is not a fixed substance but a dynamic community of love; God is being-in-relationship. The divine persons existing within the all-encompassing divine field of activity thus experience what is going on within the world of creation and are able to respond to events taking place within creation. Within every movement of experience both for God and creatures, past, present, and future coexist as ordered to one another; they are all present to and affect one another in each successive moment of eternity for the divine persons and in each successive moment of time for all creatures.[5] When we begin to understand the unfolding of trinitarian life as a dynamic process of relatedness, we can begin to accept that change in creation, including the incarnation, reflects God because change is of God. To be created is to be related, and to be related to God is to change.

THE DYNAMIC LOVE OF GOD:
BONAVENTURE AND MEISTER ECKHART

Teilhard de Chardin boldly claimed that evolution is no longer a mere hypothesis but now dominates the whole of our experience. God is conceivable only within the context of evolution. In *Christianity and Evolution* Teilhard asks, "Who will at last give evolution *its own* God?"[6] While in the case of a static world the creator is structurally independent of creation, in an evolutive world the contrary is true. God is not conceivable except insofar as God coincides with evolution (as sort of a "formal" cause) but without being lost in the center of convergence of cosmogenesis.[7] Teilhard described the God-world relationship as a twofold causality: dominant and interior. As a dominant cause among other causalities, God acts on the whole body of causes without being self-evident at any point. On the other hand, God is dynamically interior to creation, gradually bringing all things to their full being by a single creative act spanning all time.[8] Every element is an overflow of God, who makes things to make themselves.[9] God acts from within, at the core of each element, by animating the sphere of being from within. Where God is operating, it is always possible for us to see only the work of nature because God is the formal cause, the intrinsic principle of being, although God is not identical with being itself. As principle of being, God imparts to creation its inner dynamism. Because creation is essentially related to God, who is love, evolution is the unfolding process of God in love.

Although Whitehead's process theology is a twentieth-century development, writers within the Christian mystical tradition have come to similar insights, which can help renew a dynamic understanding of God. Franciscan theologian Bonaventure (1217–74) viewed creation as the outflow of divine self-giving love. Bonaventure's metaphysics of love is based on three closely related trinitarian terms: *primacy, fecundity,* and *communicability.*[10] The first divine person, the Father, he writes, is without origin and is primal and self-diffusive, the source or fountain fullness *(fontalis plenitudo)* of goodness.[11] The Son is that person eternally generated by the Father's self-diffusive goodness *(per modum naturae)*; that is, the Father naturally and necessarily communicates goodness out of the fountain fullness of goodness. As the total personal expression of the Father, the Son is Word, and as ultimate likeness to the Father, the Son is Image.[12] The Son/Word is generated by the Father, and with the Father the Son breathes forth the Spirit, who is that eternal bond of love between the Father and Son. The Spirit proceeds from the Father and Son in an act of full freedom *(per modum voluntatis)* and from a clear and determinate loving volition among them.[13]

Bonaventure's theology is centered on the divine Word. As the center of divine Life, the Word is the ontological basis for all that is other than the Father. That is, the communicability of God's nature is rooted in the primal relation between the Father and Word, which is the basis of all other relations. The centrality of the Word in Bonaventure's thought means that God is an outward-moving dynamic Trinity, whose essential life is marked by personal gift: the Father, who is *fontalis plenitudo,* gives the divine self totally by producing another, the Son, and Father and Son complete the cycle of total self-diffusion in producing the Spirit. The fecundity and dynamic life of God involve the eternal procession of love from love that exists in time and history as the missions of incarnation and deification. "Because there is a Word in God, creation can exist as an external word; because there is an Absolute Otherness, there can be a relative otherness."[14] The possibility of God's creative activity rests in his being as triune, which is to say that "God could not communicate being to the finite if he were not supremely communicative in Godself."[15] The Word, who is the center of the divine life, is exemplar of creation, and creation itself may be seen as an external word in which the one inner Word is expressed through the indwelling Spirit. Bonaventure centered the mystery of Christ in the metaphysics of divine self-relatedness that is the Trinity. The Father begets the Son through the self-communication of love, and with the Son breathes forth love in the Spirit. It is out of this creative love that all other created reality flows. Zachary Hayes writes:

> The metaphysical question coincides with the Christological question in as far as the problem of exemplarity which is focused in metaphysics at the philosophical level is related to the exemplarity of the Word incarnate in Jesus Christ. . . . God speaks but one Word in which the world and its history are co-spoken. . . . There is, however, a point in history at which the content of that Word is historicized with such explicitness that from that point light is shed on all of reality."[16]

That point is Christ the center.

Since this Word is the Word of eternal love spoken in history, it is reasonable to suggest that Bonaventure's metaphysics of Christ the center is a metaphysics of love. In light of Christ, Bonaventure views the exemplary nature of created reality not as being but as love. This insight enables Bonaventure to recast classical metaphysics in the following manner: "God is being but being is Love; God is substance but substance is relational; God is one but the highest unity is the unity of plurality in love."[17] Only when the doctrine of being is held open to the mystery of Christ is the true nature of created reality revealed as love. To say that God creates *out of love* is to say that the metaphysical basis of created being is love, since creation is patterned on the exemplary Word of love. True knowledge of created reality, therefore, is not rooted in the intellect but in love and hence is personal and relational. Emmanuel Falque writes: "Any strictly *theo*-logical truth [for Bonaventure], one that has its roots in God, will no longer be content with its unique objective determination. One the contrary, such a truth will take on a performative sense, one that is transforming for the subject that states it, or it will not exist."[18]

While Bonaventure's dynamic, relational Trinity provides a fruitful ground for a dynamic, relational universe, we find a similar notion of God in the theology of Meister Eckhart, for whom the very process of generating life defines the God-world relationship.[19] Eckhart describes creation as the eternal constant activity of God's flow into creatures. Creation is the giving of existence. Eckhart links the emanation of the universe from God with the inner procession of the persons in the Trinity through his teaching on *bullitio* and *ebullitio* ("boiling over"). Divine *bullitio* is that by which something from itself, out of itself, and in itself produces a pure nature, pouring it forth formally without the cooperation of the will but rather concomitant activity. Just as the Word exists as Logos and Image in the mind of the Father, who is principle, so "the Father speaks the Son always, in unity, and pours out in him all created things."[20] God's activity is identical with God's being; hence, creation always takes place in the simple now of eternity, and it is always new because the Word is always being born or generated by the Father.[21]

Eckhart speaks of the *grunt* or ground, the divine depth or abyss, the hidden source from which all things proceed and to which they return. This ground is the Godhead, out of which emanates the trinitarian persons, from which creation flows in turn. He poses a dialectical relation between oneness and threeness in God by asserting that the ground or Godhead is God beyond God, the hidden ground of the Trinity, the One who by the very nature of being One, swells, boils up, and is infinitely fecund. He writes: "Life bespeaks a type of pushing out by which something swells up in itself and first breaks out totally in itself, each part into each part, before it pours itself forth and boils over on the outside *(ebulliat)*."[22] Eckhart describes *bullitio* as a "breaking out and the first breakout or melting forth is where God liquefies and where he melts into his Son and where the Son melts back into the Father."[23] His *bullitio* can be likened to Bonaventure's notion of the Father as unoriginate-fountain fullness. The dialectical nature of the Father or the One is the basis of boiling or overflowing into the Word, expressing this overflowing love in the Spirit.[24] Just as the Word exists as Logos, Idea, and Image in the mind of the Father who is the Word's Principle, so too that Logos serves as the exemplary cause by which God creates. Since God's Word has been spoken from all eternity, indeed, is being spoken from all eternity (God as Father must always be uttering the Word, who is Son), then the virtual existence of all things, when viewed in the Principle, is always being spoken by the Father in the one and the same eternal act in which the Father speaks the Word. Although God's continuous act of creation means that in its deepest reality creation is eternal, Eckhart did not deny that the universe is also temporal, that is, something made in time (since time itself is created.) He emphasized, however, that God's creative activity always takes place in the present; hence, God's action is always new, for God is always creating anew.

THE EMERGENT GOD

Bonaventure and Meister Eckhart speak to us of a God who is dynamic, relational, communal, and transcendent in love. Whereas Eckhart distinguished between Godhead and God, and thus between Godhead and Trinity, Bonaventure made no such distinction. Rather, he saw the negative pole of the Father's infinite unbegottenness as the complement to the positive pole of the Father's Fountain fullness. Both theologians claim that boiling up or fountain fullness constitutes the ground or first principle. For Bonaventure, being is goodness, and the highest good is love, which, by nature, is transcendent. What constitutes the Father, therefore, is not simply being the first divine person but the primacy of dynamic self-communicative love. In the one eternal-temporal dynamic act of love, every "boiling up" of the Father, which is the Word, is a boiling over into creation or Word incarnate. The boiling over of the Word into creation means that what takes place in finite creation reflects the dynamic trinitarian communion of fecund love. Since the trinitarian communion of love is the ground of creation, creation takes place within the drama of trinitarian life. The dynamic divine life is the environment in which the universe is brought to life and empowered to unfold. As Denis Edwards writes, "The universe can be understood as unfolding 'within' the Trinitarian relations of mutual love."[25]

For Bonaventure and Eckhart, the mystery of God lies in the dialectic of the first divine person, who is infinite in origin and overflowing in nature. The Father is origin or source of divine personal love and is Father only in relation to the Son, who is everything the Father is in one other than the Father. The person of the Father is marked by the constant flow of love—from no other *(non ab alio)* into one other; from unoriginate to originate; from emptiness to fullness. The Father is what we might call a *singularity*, an indeterminate beginning of God that is itself without beginning.[26] Just as a singularity marks the beginning of our evolutionary universe, so too the singularity of the first divine person marks the "beginning" of emergent trinitarian life. As the beginning without beginning, the Father has a dialectical nature in which newness identifies the fountain fullness. The dialectical nature of the Primal One undergirds the Father becoming other by sharing/diffusing of self, and it is in becoming other in the Son that the Father is truly Father. Although the Son is everything the Father is in one other than the Father, the Son cannot be reduced to the Father. On the contrary, the Son is all that the Father is and yet more than the Father by the nature of the Father's self-expressive love. Similarly, the communicative dynamic love between the Father and Son is a union of love in the Spirit. Just as the Son cannot be reduced to the Father, neither can the Spirit be reduced to the Father or the Son. Rather, the Spirit is more than the union of Father and Son because it is the union between Father and Son that breathes forth the Spirit. Hence, the Spirit of divine love is exhaled as the absolute "more" of God's eternal love. The Spirit not only expresses perfect union in love but because divine love is eternally generated by the newness of love between the Father and Son, the Spirit signifies the horizon of becoming in love.

The relational life of the Trinity is not a static communion but a dynamic flow of love, love unto love or, we might say, a nested hierarchy of loves—generative, expressive, and unitive loves. The Trinity is eternal flowing love, whereby the love of one to another—Father to Son to Spirit—is a complexified union of love in which each divine person recapitulates the generation of love as a new horizon. What is said of Alfred Whitehead's God can be said here as well: "The Father at any given moment is not precisely the same as the 'Father' of the preceding moment, and the same may be said of the 'Son' and the 'Spirit' in the successive moments of their existence."[27] The eternal, dynamic unfolding of trinitarian persons is the eternal, dynamic unfolding God: God is always becoming God. Or, we might say that God is always evolving. The infinite, incomprehensible, utterly fecund One is always becoming a plurality in love; yet, it is precisely the plurality of persons-in-love that renders God unity in love. As Eckhart wrote: "When we say God is eternal we mean God is eternally young. . . . God is the newest thing there is, the youngest thing there is. God is the beginning and if we are united to God we become new again."[28] Although Bonaventure used the term *circumincessio* to describe the mutual indwelling of the three divine persons, we can envision this indwelling not as three persons sitting around one another or a divine dance but the movement from within to be for another so as to become more in the other. The emergent Trinity may be described as love yielding to love, an eternal movement toward personal, complexified union in love. Thus every divine person is nested in every other person so that every divine person recapitulates God, who is eternally coming to be. God is that than which no greater is coming to be for it is in the coming to be that God is.

GOD: NOUN OR VERB?

If the Trinity is a nested hierarchy of loves or a holarchy of love whereby the Spirit signifies the eternal horizon of love, then newness defines God; every act of the Trinity is an eternal new beginning in love. This dynamic nature of God as love demands a new language with *God* not as absolute subject but as absolute verb. David Cooper in *God Is a Verb: Kabbalah and the Practice of Mystical Judaism* highlights a continuous problem, the meaning of "Ego sum," the "I AM" of God. His basic question is ours as well. If God shares life with us so that all creation is the oozing life of God, can God simply "be" an uninvolved substance than which no greater can be thought? Cooper answers this question by saying that God is not a noun but a verb—an interactive verb. Cooper suggests that "Godding" is a mutually interactive verb that entails an interdependency between two subjects, each being the object for the other.[29] If God is a verb, then can we speak of the Trinity not as a noun but as a verb as well? Perhaps we can say God is a noun-verb, the One who trinitizes and hence ecologizes the world through active, creative, boiling over, diffusive relationships of love—the interrelated, unbroken wholeness within which the wholeness of creation exists as a quantum event, the coincidence of divine love. God is ecstatic loving relationship, infinitely flowing from oneness to threeness, from source to perfection, from singularity to plurality. God is infinite fecundity, depth, movement, process, and relatedness. The Trinity is the constant emerging novelty of divine love whereby "loving" always forms the horizon of ever-deepening love. If *Trinity* means the horizon of God as love, then we can speak of God's dynamic life not as first cause or origin of Being, that is, the Godhead, but as the horizon of all that is and coming to be, the God Ahead. God is the newness of everything that is and is coming to be. God is ever newness in love. Transcendence, therefore, is the future beyond that draws us in the present movement toward greater wholeness and unity.

By shifting our thinking of God from noun to verb, from Godhead to God Ahead, we see that God is another name for novelty, an idea that complements Karl Rahner's notion of God as absolute future. In evolution, Rahner claims, what *is* clearly *becomes something altogether new*, as in the emergence of self-conscious human beings. Thus, as Denis Edwards claims, God must be understood "not simply as the dynamic cause of the existence of creatures, but as the dynamic ground of their becoming."[30] Rahner says, according to Edwards, that we need to think of the divine act of ongoing creation not simply as the divine "conservation" and "concursus" of all things, but *as the enabling of creation to become what is radically new*, what he calls "active self-transcendence."[31] According to Rahner, God empowers creation from within to transcend itself and become more than what it was.[32] This is the biblical view of God, a God of promise and hope or, as Wolfhart Pannenberg states, the "power of the future."[33] This God of the future *is* the God of the present; God is future-present because God who comes to us from the future is the horizon of our becoming and the power of our coming to be.

Teilhard de Chardin recognized that a God of evolution must be a God who is "less Alpha than Omega." He felt that the traditional view of God and creation, the "metaphysics of the eternally present," was inadequate for the reality of evolution. Evolution, he claimed, requires a divine source located not in the past or "up above" in a timeless present but "up ahead" in the future. He described the God of the future, the God "up ahead," as the ultimate force of attraction for the universe, drawing the universe toward intensification of complexity and new creation.[34] If the Trinity is eternally self-expressive dynamic overflowing love—love unto love—then the future is marked by the horizon of love. In this way we can speak of evolutionary creation as progress toward ultimate love in relationship to a God of ever-deepening love.

To think of the triune God residing in the future is to think of God as the horizon of love. By *future* I do not mean the unknown or the not-yet; rather, future pertains to the *plenum* of divine potentialities, all the possibilities that can be realized through grace. God "is the transcendent future horizon that draws an entire universe, and not just human history, toward an unfathomable fulfillment yet to be realized."[35] The Trinity speaks to us of novelty and future; it embraces and sustains the world at the cusp where the future meets the present, where the "not-yet" stands on the threshold of the "now." If the power of divine love that is the dynamic emergent triune God is source and goal of all that is, then we can speak of the fidelity of divine love in an evolutionary universe as the transcendent source of change. God is ever newness in love, eternally becoming God in love unto love.

Chapter Three

Creative Union

If the story of creation is the story of God, then we have a slight problem, because in this story there is no original perfection or Garden of Eden from which humans fell into sin. Rather, it is a wild, unpredictable, and unruly universe in which God emerges in the human person, Jesus of Nazareth. How do we understand the significance of Jesus Christ in the ongoing process of evolution? This is a challenging question because the word *evolution* disarms the formula of Jesus Christ described by the Council of Chalcedon in AD 451. The fathers of the church worked with the physics and philosophy of their day, grappling with the terms *nature, substance,* and *person* to arrive at an understanding of Jesus Christ that would last for centuries:

> The same Christ, Son, Lord, Only-begotten, recognized in two natures, without confusion, without change, without division, without separation; the distinction of natures being in no way annulled by the union, but rather the characteristics of each nature being preserved and coming together to form one person and subsistence . . . one and the same Son and Only-begotten God the Word, Lord Jesus Christ.[1]

If relationship rather than substance better describes the nature of material reality today, how do we understand the person of Jesus Christ as a union of divine and human natures? What is substance or nature in view of quantum physics, chaos theory, and complexity? In light of quantum physics and evolution, is it helpful to speak of Christ in terms of two natures or is there another way of understanding Christ more fitting to the cosmic reality we find ourselves in?

F. Leron Shults states that we need a total reconstruction of Christology today if it is to be credible for our world.[2] Christ cannot be the great exception to the world; rather, if Christ is Word made flesh, then this incarnate Word must be the innermost meaning of the world in evolution. We need to revisit the meaning of Jesus Christ in the context of an evolutionary creation. Can we understand the person of Jesus as the evolutionary divine emergent in history, not only as the mysterious union of natures, but as the integrated being in whom a new field of activity arises that promotes wholeness and evolution toward God? Can we see Jesus as the exemplar of relatedness for the fullness of evolutionary life?

To explore the meaning of Jesus Christ in evolution, it is helpful to keep several ideas in mind. The first is that creation and incarnation are not two separate events but one process of God's self-giving and self-communication. When we talk about the incarnation, we are also talking about creation. The God who creates is the God who saves because salvation *is* new creation. Second, whatever we say about creation, we are saying about God. Creation expresses the Creator; it is an outward expression of God's love and grace. Creation is the book that tells us about God, because God is the author of creation. Third, God is dynamic, trinitarian love, which means that love is the source, meaning, and goal of creation. Love is not added on to creation, like an outer coat of paint that makes creation nice and pretty; rather, love defines created reality. If quantum physics indicates that matter is energy-in-relationship, then from a theological perspective, matter-energy is love or ultimate goodness.

EVOLUTION AND CREATIVE UNION

While classical theology viewed creation as a free act of God, either by way of desire (Bonaventure) or intellect (Thomas), Teilhard de Chardin saw creation as integral to God. He believed that without creation, something would be absolutely lacking in God, considered in the fullness not of God's being but of God's act of union. The history of the universe is a sacred story in sacred time. It is a story of God who comes to be in what God is not. Creation always bears in its innermost being a divine relation, and yet it is not divine. God is the future *plenum* of all that can be, and yet God is dynamically interior to creation, gradually bringing all things to their full being by a single creative act spanning all time.[3] Because creation is relationship, God acts from within, at the core of each element, by animating the sphere of being from within. God, therefore, imparts to creation its inner dynamism of love and hence relationality. Christopher Mooney writes:

> The assertion that the world's movement towards unity "completes" God in some way is unusual and needs to be clarified. . . . Teilhard is doing nothing more nor less than asserting in an evolutionary context the paradox which is already contained in St. Paul: *the Pleroma of Christ cannot constitute an intrinsic completion of God himself,* but it will nonetheless in some sense be a real completion. . . . Teilhard wants to do away once and for all with the idea that God's continuous act of creation is one of *absolute* gratuity.[4]

For Teilhard, the relationality of God's triune nature makes creation more than an act willed out of intellect or desire; creation is the truly beloved of God and hence fulfills God's desire for relationship. He opposed the idea of an absolutely gratuitous creation because it makes creation inferior to God rather than a partner with the divine. Creation, in a sense, complements God, not by supplying something God lacks, but by relating to what God is as divine love. It is the completion of creation as *pleroma* that God desires, because the completion of creation is the fullness of God (cf. 1 Cor 15:28). God participates in creation because God is dynamic, relational being whose openness to relationship is the basis of evolution. If God was not triune, we could not conceive the possibility of God creating (or being incarnate) without totally immersing Godself in the world God brings into being.[5]

Teilhard described the incarnation as "creative union," a process of immanent unification in which Christ is in process of being created by the gradual unification of multiplicity. Thus "creation" is to be located not at the "beginning" of the world but at its "end." Creation emerges with evolution as lower level entities become higher level entities with a persistent emergence of novelty whereby each unification results in new being.[6] By uniting the processes of

evolution and creative union, Teilhard showed that he was less concerned with being and becoming than with the relationship between unity and multiplicity. Rather than following the classic metaphysical construct of the many flowing from the One (a devolution
or thinning out of being), Teilhard posited that the One flows from
the many (a building up toward the fullness of being). The involve-
ment of God in evolution through creative union means that everything happens as though the One were formed by successive
unifications of the multiple, and as though the One were more perfect the more perfectly it centralized under itself a larger multiple.[7]
The One appears to us only in the midst of the multiple, dominat-
ing the multiple, since its essential act is to unite. God is revealed
everywhere as a universal milieu, only because God is the ultimate
point upon which all realities converge. For Teilhard, the new
evolutive God rises up at the heart of the old maker-God, for if
God had not pre-emerged from the world, then God could not be
for the world.[8]

Teilhard believed that God could not appear as prime mover
without first becoming incarnate and without redeeming—in other
words *without our seeing that he becomes christified*.[9] The observation
in nature of greater unity, from atoms to cells to plants to animals
and humans, led him to posit a centrating factor, a basis of unity
that is both immanent and transcendent to material reality. The
unity of the Trinity is the Center or Word of God who flows from
the fontal love of the Father. The Father's self-expressed love is
centered in the Word; hence, when God turns toward the world,
Christ becomes the center of creation. The Trinity shows the essential condition of God's capacity to be the personal summit of a
universe that is in the process of personalization. It is not surpris-
ing that when Teilhard discovered the doctrine of the primacy of
Christ in the Franciscan theologian Duns Scotus, he exclaimed,
"Voilà! La theologie de l'avenir" [the theology of the future].[10] His
doctrine of creative union complemented the Franciscan idea that
Christ is first in God's intention to love.[11] For Teilhard, evolution
is aimed at divinity from the beginning, and the christified universe is always its goal.[12]

Teilhard used the term *christogenesis* to indicate that the biological and cosmological genesis of creation is, from the point of faith,
christogenesis. By *genesis* he indicated that evolution involves directed

change, organized becoming, patterned process, cumulative order. It is not mere change or becoming which can be random, disordered, and meaningless. Rather, evolution has direction. Teilhard recognized that there is a unifying influence in the whole evolutionary process, a centrating factor that continues to hold the entire process together and moves it forward toward greater complexity and unity. The ultimate mover of the entire cosmogenesis is something that is simultaneously *within* the sequence of beings as tendency, desire, and purpose, and *in front of* the advancing wave of development, beckoning it, as its ideal culmination. He identified this prime mover with God. As he indicated, classical theology assumed that God could be located "above," but now we realize that God can be located "ahead" and "within" as well.[13]

Teilhard's faith in Christ led him to posit Christ, the future fullness of the whole evolutionary process, as the "centrating principle," the "pleroma" and "Omega point" where the individual and collective adventure of humanity finds its end and fulfillment. He wrote:

> The universal Christ could not appear at the end of time at the peak of the world if he had not previously entered it during its development, through the medium of birth, in the form of an element. If it is indeed true that it is through Christ Omega that the universe-in-movement holds together, then it is from his concrete historical life, Jesus of Nazareth, that Christ-Omega derives his whole consistence, as a hard experiential fact. The two terms are intrinsically one whole, and they cannot vary in a truly total Christ except simultaneously.[14]

Christ is not an intrusion into an otherwise evolutionary universe, but its its very reason and goal.

CHRIST THE EVOLVER

Teilhard insisted that it is time to return to a form of Christology that is more organic and takes account of physics. We need a Christ "who is no longer master of the world solely because he has been *proclaimed* to be such," he wrote, "but because he animates the whole range of things from top to bottom."[15] The greatness of Teilhard's thought lies in the organic nature of Christ as the heart of change in the universe. "If we are to remain faithful to the gospel, we have to adjust its spiritual code to the new shape of the universe. It has ceased to be the formal garden from which we are temporarily banished by a whim of the Creator. It has become the great work in process of completion which we have to save by saving ourselves."[16] The most fundamental task of our age is to forge a union between evolution and Christianity, if we are to go forward toward the fullness of God. It became increasingly evident to Teilhard that if Christ is to remain at the center of our faith in an evolutionary universe, then this cosmic Christ must begin to offer himself for our adoration as the "evolutive" Christ—Christ the Evolver.[17] The *one who is in evolution* is himself the *cause and center* of evolution and its goal.

Teilhard viewed Christ as a dynamic impulse within humanity (and nonhumanity), which is moving toward greater complexity and unity, from biogenesis to noogenesis, from simple biological structures to the emergence of mind. Teilhard's Christ the Evolver is one with Christ Omega, since it is from Jesus of Nazareth that Christ Omega derives his whole consistence. The link between Christ the Evolver and Christ the Omega means that the cosmic goal is disclosed by creative union. As Evolver, Christ is that which is coming to be in evolution through the process of creative union. As Omega, Christ is superpersonal in nature—the One who fills all things and who animates and gathers up all the biological and spiritual energies developed by the universe.[18] When Teilhard spoke of Christ the Evolver, he meant that divine love is at the heart of creation and that the movement toward the fullness of love incarnate is the Christ who is coming to be. This is the very process of creation itself in evolution. Since Christ is Omega, the universe is physically impregnated to the very core of its matter by the influence of his superhuman nature. The presence of the incarnate Word penetrates everything as a universal element through grace. Everything is physically "christified," gathered up by the incarnate Word "as nourishment that assimilates, transforms, and divinizes."[19] Christ is present in the entire cosmos, from the least particle of matter to the convergent human community. The whole cosmos is incarnational. Christ is the instrument, the center, the end of the whole of animate and material creation; through him, everything is created, sanctified, and vivified. Christ invests himself organically with all of creation, immersing himself in things, in the heart of matter, and thus unifying the world.[20] By taking on human form, Christ has given the world its definitive form: he has been consecrated for a cosmic function. Christ is the fullness of nature's evolving unity in God.

Teilhard posited a dynamic view of God and the world in the process of becoming *something more* than it is because the universe is grounded in the personal *center of Christ*. Every act of evolving nature is the self-expression of God, since the very act of nature's transcendence is the energy of divine love. God unfolds in the details of nature; thus, evolution is not only *of* God but *is* God incarnate. In *Phenomenon of Man* Teilhard described evolution as an unfolding process of *withinness* and *withoutness*. The *within* is the mental aspect and the *without* is the physical aspect of the same stuff. Although this relationship between within and without points to the role of consciousness at the heart of matter, I think it also points to the simultaneous unfolding of God and world: God is the *withinness* of the *withoutness* of matter in evolution.[21] God is dynamically relational, trinitizing creation, and the trinitization of creation is, at the same time, personalizing it in Christ. Divine love is the energy of trinitization because love is dynamic, and dynamic love is never the same from moment to moment. What Teilhard pointed to is that divine love is evolutionary—it changes, grows, complexifies—and this growth and complexification is the basis of unity. Even in human relations, the perfection of love comes at the end of a long, loving relationship, not in the beginning. In *Christianity and Evolution* Teilhard said that "the universe is finally and permanently unified only through personal relations (that is, under the influence of love). . . . The elements of the world become more themselves, the more they converge on God."[22] God is not the source of love in creation; rather, love (the divine, creative intrinsic principle) is the source of God in creation; God emerges out of relationships of love. Karl Rahner wrote, "God is not merely the one who as creator establishes a world distant from himself as something different, but rather he is the one who gives himself away to this world and who has his own fate in and with this world. God is not only himself the giver, but he is also the gift."[23] That is, God is the core of the world's reality and the world is the "fate" of God.[24]

EVOLUTION AND INCARNATION

Whereas classical theology begins with the philosophical notion of being and the existence of God, Teilhard began with the
science of evolution and hence of God. The creative union of God-
matter by which all of matter is spiritualized reaches its culmination in Jesus of Nazareth, in whom the direction of evolution is
revealed. In *Christianity and Evolution* Teilhard wrote that the early
church sought to understand Christ's relation to the Trinity. However, "in our own time the vitally important question has become
for us to define the links between Christ and the universe: how
they stand in relation to one another and how they influence one
another."[25] What Teilhard tried to show is that evolution is not
only the universe coming to be but it is *God* who is *coming to be*. His
radical thought is twofold: suffering, pain, and death are part of an
evolutionary universe (not the result of original sin), and Christ is
the fullness *(pleroma)* of that which is coming to be. Thus he states,
"God is entirely self-sufficient; and yet the universe contributes
something that is vitally necessary to him."[26] Teilhard felt that the traditional view of God and creation, the "metaphysics of the eternally present," was inadequate for the reality of evolution. Evolution, he claimed, requires a divine source located not in the past or
"up above" in a timeless present but "up ahead" in the future. Thus
he suggests that a metaphysics of *Being* be replaced by a metaphysics of *Unity* since unity marks evolution and, in creation, the evolution of multiplicity is unitive. In a footnote to *Christianity and Evolution* he writes:

> We might say that for the discursive reason two phases can be
> distinguished in "theogenesis." In the first, God posits him-
> self in his Trinitarian structure ("fontal" being reflecting it-
> self, self-sufficient, upon itself): "Trinitization." In the sec-
> ond phase, he envelops himself in participated being, by
> evolutive unification of pure multiple (positive non-being)
> born (in a state of absolute potency) by antithesis to pre-pos-
> ited Trinitarian unity: Creation.[27]

Rather than following a classical, static theology of God-world
relationship, in which the end returns to the beginning *(Omega*

revolvit ad alpha), Teilhard reframes the God-world relationship from the point of evolution. "The organic vastness of the universe," he states, "obliges us to rethink the notion of divine *omnisufficiency*: God fulfills himself, he in some way completes himself, in the pleroma."[28] Thus evolution reveals a newness to God. Just as novelty marks "being-in-evolution," so too novelty marks "God-in-evolution." Whereas traditional theology postulates God as *cause* of all things, Teilhard postulates God as the *goal* toward which all things are moving. He described the God of the future, the God "up ahead," as the ultimate force of attraction for the universe, drawing the universe toward intensification of complexity and new creation. If the Trinity is eternally self-expressive dynamic overflowing love—love unto love—then the future is marked by the horizon of love. In this way we can speak of evolutionary creation as progress toward ultimate love in relationship to a God of ever-deepening love.

Teilhard viewed evolution and incarnation as interrelated; the God-matter creative union means that creation can only have one object: a *universe*, that is, creation "can be effected only by an *evolutive process* (of personalizing synthesis) and that it can come into action *only once*: when absolute multiple is reduced, nothing is left to be united either in God or 'outside' God."[29] We might call this idea the primacy of Christ in evolution. If Christ is the goal of God's intention to love, then evolution is a single act of trinitarian love because the heart of God is reflected in the heart of the world. Evolution, therefore, is a single act of love in space-time, a trinitizing of creation and thus a unifying personalization in Christ. That is why incarnation does not take place *in* evolution; Christ does not intervene in creation and then become its goal. Rather, the whole evolutionary process is incarnational. Evolution is *christogenesis* or God coming to be at the heart of matter, but it is also *theogenesis* because it is *God* coming to be at the heart of matter. In Teilhard's view it is not something but *Someone* who holds together the plurality of elements in a personalizing center, and this is Christ.[30] God can only create evolutively, Teilhard states, because the whole point of creation is the fullness of love personalized in Christ, the unitive center of creation.[31] As the Evolver, Christ is the one in evolution; as Omega Point, Christ holds together the universe in movement. Instead of seeing creation *return* to the Father, Teilhard identifies the Father in relation to the Son as the one who vitalizes and engenders. Every theological development that "affects the theology of the Son-Object-of-Love must affect the Father in whom all being must ultimately find its source."[32] Thus if Christ the Word incarnate is in evolution, it is because the Father is in evolution as well, the one who makes possible the dynamism of love. As the infinite, transcendent source of love, God is up ahead, the God of the future who draws the universe toward a new future of creative union. John Haught expounds Teilhard's thought by saying that God "is the transcendent future horizon that draws an entire universe, and not just human history, toward an unfathomable fulfillment yet to be realized."[33] Evolution is progress toward union in love because God is ever-deepening love.

JESUS AND THE POWER OF NEWNESS

Teilhard did not believe that the human reality of Jesus Christ was lost in the superhuman and vanished in the cosmic. If Christ is the centrating principle of evolution, the personal center of this cosmic process, then this center emerges as something new in the person of Jesus of Nazareth. The new science of emergence holds particular interest in this dynamic world view marked by evolution and complexity. "In ordinary language emergence refers to processes of coming forth from latency, or to states of things arising unexpectedly."[34] Philip Clayton defines emergence as "genuinely new properties which are not reducible to what came before, although they are continuous with it."[35] In *Mind and Emergence* Clayton writes: "Emergent properties are those that arise out of some subsystem but are not reducible to that system. Emergence is about *more than but not altogether other than*. . . . Emergence means that the world exhibits a recurrent pattern of novelty and irreducibility."[36] Denis Edwards describes emergence as something that is constituted from components in such a way that it has new properties that are not reducible to the properties of the components.[37] Niels Henrik Gregersen notes that emergence theory was formed as a meta-scientific interpretation of evolution in all its forms— cosmic, biological, mental, and cultural—by British scientists in the 1920s. Although emergentists differ in metaphysical orientation, he writes, they usually share three tenets: (1) Emergents are qualitative novelties that should be distinguished from mere resultants, which come about by a quantitative addition of parts (weight, for example, is an aggregate of matter, whereas water emerges from the combination of compounds, hydrogen and oxygen, and is composed of but different from them). (2) Nature is a nested hierarchy of ontological levels, so that the higher emergent levels include the lower levels on which they are based. (3) Higher levels are not predictable from our knowledge of their constituent parts, and their operations are often in principle irreducible to the lower levels.[38] The mark of emergence is *irreducible novelty* which pertains not only to the properties of the new emerging entity but to the entity itself as new. What we can say about emergence is that "the whole is more than the sum of its parts," so that constitutive characteristics are not explainable from the characteristics of the isolated parts. Rather, emergent life in the universe is marked by the appearance of the radically new.

Teilhard de Chardin said that the Christ event brings a new directionality into evolution, beginning with the human person, who is the growing tip of the evolutionary movement. The newness of Jesus initiates a continuing drama and dialectic in the history of the world; human life and history take on a new theological intensity. Jesus enters the evolutionary trajectory bringing all *newness* in himself. A *power of newness* comes into the human person, into the heart and mind: a new *creativity* that is divine and human at once. As the one who brings a new consciousness of love into the universe, Christ is a new centrating factor who holds the entire process together and moves it forward toward greater complexity and unity.

Jesus Christ is not the great exception to the universe but the climax of a long development whereby the world becomes aware of itself and comes into the direct presence of God.[39] The body of Jesus, like every human body, is made from cosmic dust birthed in the interior of ancient stars that long predated our planet and solar system. The iron that ran through his veins, the phosphorus and calcium that fortified his bones, the sodium and potassium that facilitated the transmission of signals through his nerves—all make the incarnation a truly cosmic event. Jesus participated in the unfolding of life and the emergence of consciousness, just like any other human being; his humanity is our humanity, and his cosmic earthly life is ours as well.

However, in Jesus something new emerges, a new consciousness, a new relatedness, and a new immediacy of God's presence—

in short—a new Big Bang. Jesus Christ symbolizes a new unity in creation: non-duality, reconciling love, healing mercy, and compassion. Jesus brings a "new heart" to humanity, both on the individual and the collective planes. Humanity becomes a new "creative center" within the evolutionary process in such a way that the path of this evolution now becomes explicitly directed; evolution has a goal. William Thompson suggests that a new level of consciousness was initiated by Jesus and the early Christian community. Following John Cobb, he writes that "in Jesus we find the Hebraic ethically responsible individual and the intense experience of God's immediacy, simultaneously. . . . Jesus' sense of divine immediacy resulted in a present experience of the kingdom." Thompson then states: "Jesus radicalized the Hebraic entry into axial consciousness. . . . [His] death glaringly sums up what such a consciousness entails, and forever manifests that the style of life characteristic of radical God-centeredness is not the negation of this-worldly responsibility, but its intensification to the furthest limits. The suffering and death of Jesus were a radical manifestation that faith in God liberates the individual to accept the full implications of his freedom and responsibility."[40] The awareness of God's immediacy and a sense of ethical responsibility (for example, feed the hungry, clothe the naked, compassion for the poor) marked the new Christian consciousness.

Thompson claims that "Jesus' ministry and resurrection brought the process of human spiritualization to its completion and removed every barrier to its complete emergence."[41] In some way the empowering presence of God activated and heightened an individual's self-responsibility; for example, Paul found himself capable of confronting every imaginable obstacle: death, life, the powers of the cosmos, present and future, and every living creature (Rom 8:35–39). This heightened sense of self-responsibility meant a heightened freedom. Through the work of the Spirit one was free from the law and could live on a new level of existence, free from the oppressive powers of this world and from the past. One could now live in a reality that radically transcended and rationalized them.[42] What emerged in Jesus was the immediacy of God's presence and, in his death and resurrection, the power of God's presence to conquer all forces threatening to destroy not only human individuation but human relatedness. In Jesus there emerged a new sense of what it means to belong to the cosmos.

GOD'S CREATIVE AIM

To talk about Jesus as the person of radically new consciousness within history puts a new emphasis on the purpose of the incarnation. Since the eleventh century Western Christology has held fast to sin as the primary reason for Christ. Anselm of Canterbury said that the incarnation was necessary to repay the debt due because of the sin of Adam and Eve. At Easter we proclaim "O Happy Fault" because if Adam had not sinned, Christ would not have come. Although Western Christology has focused on sin as the reason for Christ, there is no reference to Adam and Eve anywhere else in the Hebrew Bible (nor does Jesus ever refer to them!), which has led scholars to conclude "that the story was added relatively late in Israel's history in response to creation myths of its ancient Near Eastern neighbors."[43] Similarly, the story of the virgin birth does not appear in the earliest Gospel of Mark and seems to have no effect on Jesus' self-identity or teaching.[44] As Shults indicates, it is time to loosen Christology from a literal reading of Genesis and a particular biological understanding of the virgin birth. Such loosening, however, does not deny sin; rather it is to refocus the incarnation in its theological context and not its anthropological fixation on sin. Seeing the incarnation as the emergence of God in the history of the universe, that is, the inner pressure of love at the heart of the universe, gives new meaning to evolution and to sin as part of an evolutionary world.

If the nature of love is unity and evolution is process toward greater unity, then sin is resistance to unity. Hildegard of Bingen described sin as living in the exile of unrelatedness; it is the refusal to change and grow. Sin, we might say, is the refusal to participate in the web of life. It describes the personal history of one who was created for communion and refuses it.[45] It is, as Jane Kopas says, the rejection of our identity as part of an interdependent world in which God's power as creative source expresses itself through shared power of other creatures.[46] Sin is the refusal to accept responsibility for those to whom we are connected; thus, it is the refusal to accept the "other" of relationship (the "Thou") as the one who addresses us, discloses our responsibility, and calls us into question.[47] It signifies the current alienation of nature from humanity, its estrangement from God and from its own creative possibilities envisaged by God from the outset of creation.[48] Sin is the refusal to be a person of true relationship, which results in a broken human community and in abandonment of the natural world. The desire to overcome sin, according to Hayes, is the desire to overcome all obstacles that stand in the way of the accomplishment of God's creative aim, which is the fullest possible sharing of life and love between God and creation.[49]

Although sin may be part of the evolutionary process as resistance or conflict within the process, it does not thwart the divine energy that empowers evolution toward wholeness. If God is the heart of evolution and Christ is coming to be, then grace is everywhere. God's gracious love sustains the evolutionary movement toward ever-deepening life. Jesus bursts forth on the evolutionary scene not because of sin but because of love. God's love comes to explicit awareness in the person of Jesus of Nazareth. Humanity becomes a new "creative center" within the cosmic process in such a way that the cosmos has a goal; it is not an eternal cycle of life and death but oriented toward a new future. Jesus ushers in a whole new understanding of heaven and earth. In a sense, he shatters the ancient cosmos with its layers of spiritual and material reality by announcing a new unity of heaven and earth. No longer is God reigning over the celestial domes. Now God is present in history, in the everyday world of life. Looking back from our own time, we can say that the purpose of evolution appears in the life of Jesus Christ. His radical new way of life anticipates what will take two thousand more years for science to discover, that life in the universe evolves toward greater unity, a process that encompasses suffering, death, and new life. Jesus' entire life points toward a new future in God.

Chapter Four

Jesus the Whole-Maker

As a new religion, Christianity lived on the margins of a pagan Roman culture and struggled to spread its message of God's indwelling love to all the world. Jesus had commissioned his disciples: "Go therefore, and make disciples of all nations, baptizing them in the name of the Father and of the Son and of the Holy Spirit, teaching them to observe all that I have commanded you" (Mt 28:19–20). In the early days of Christianity, prior to the age of Constantine, to be a Christian meant accepting costly discipleship. Christians, like Jesus, were willing to give their life for the sake of the gospel. It was one of these early martyrs, Ignatius of Antioch, who is usually credited with first using the term *catholic* in his letter to the Smyrnaeans (ca. 107–10).[1] Throughout his letters Ignatius tried to preserve the core of Christian theology. He taught the divinity of Christ, the Eucharist as medicine of immortality, the relationship between bishop and church, and was the first to use the Greek word *katholikos*, meaning "according to [*kata-*] the whole [*holos*]," or more colloquially, "universal." John Haughey writes, "The term *catholicity* promises a worldview that is universal in classical Greek; *kata* (a preposition) and *holos* (a noun) when coupled become *kath' holou*, an adverb meaning 'wholly' and *katholikos*, a substantive that is best rendered 'catholicity' in English."[2] The word *catholic* describes movement toward universality or wholeness. Walter Ong offers an interpretation of the word *catholic* that helps us understand it in light of Jesus' mission:

> "Catholic" is commonly said to mean "universal," a term from the Latin *universalis*. The equation is not quite exact. If

"universal" is the adequate meaning of "catholic" why did the Latin church, which in its vernacular language had the word *universalis*, not use the word but rather borrowed from the Greek the term *katholikos* instead, speaking of the "one, holy, catholic and apostolic church" instead of the "one, holy, universal and apostolic church"?[3]

Ong states that universality is not an inclusive concept because everything that is not in the circle of universality is excluded from it. The word *catholic*, however, simply means "through-the-whole" or "throughout-the-whole," like yeast that leavens bread. The word *catholic* connotes an active presence of "whole-making" or leavening the stuff of life to create a greater whole. It is interesting that the word *catholic* emerged after the death of Jesus to describe the church as the one true body of Christ by those seeking to spread the faith amid a hostile environment. The word *church* comes from the Greek *ecclesia*, which means "those called out," as in those called to be "whole-makers" in the world. By the third century the term *catholic* was used to describe the nature of Christ's mystical body, the church, less as a process of "whole-making" than as a mark of true orthodoxy. In the letter to the Smyrnaeans, Ignatius wrote: "Wherever the bishop appears, there let the multitude be; even as wherever Christ Jesus is, there is the Catholic Church."[4]

The martyrdom account of Polycarp, Bishop of Smyrna, also speaks of the Catholic Church, linking the bishop with the church and martyrdom as true witness to the faith. The authors write that as his martyrdom was consummated with fire and sword, Polycarp's spirit was released like incense, thus showing him to be a true apostolic and prophetic teacher, "bishop of the holy church in Smyrna." The authors continue: "Such is the story of the blessed Polycarp. . . . He proved to be not only a distinguished teacher, but also an outstanding martyr, whose martyrdom all desire to imitate since it was in accord with the pattern of the gospel of Christ. . . . Now he rejoices with the apostles and all the righteous . . . and blesses our Lord Jesus Christ . . . Shepherd of the catholic church throughout the whole world."[5] The martyrdom accounts of Ignatius and Polycarp show that early Christians held that where the bishop is, so too is the church, because the role of the bishop is to preserve the unity of the church. The church is to be gathered together into a single body through Jesus Christ. "Just as this broken bread was scattered upon the mountains and then was gathered together and became one, so may your church be gathered together from the ends of the earth into your kingdom."[6]

While early Christians used the word *catholic* to distinguish orthodoxy from heresy, it was not confined to this distinction. In his "Catechetical Discourses," Cyril of Jerusalem used the word *catholic* in its literal meaning: "Now it [the church] is called Catholic because it is throughout the world, from one end of the earth to the other."[7] The word *catholic* was included in the Roman Creed by the fourth century and affirmed the one, true apostolic church. Historian of the early church J. N. D. Kelly writes:

> As regards "catholic," its original meaning was "universal" or "general." . . . In the latter half of the second century at latest, we find it conveying the suggestion that the Catholic is the true Church as distinct from heretical congregations. . . . What these early Fathers were envisaging was almost always the empirical, visible society; they had little or no inkling of the distinction which was later to become important between a visible and an invisible Church."[8]

While the early fathers used the word *catholic* to describe the church, they did so in a hostile environment in which the young, fragile religion was threatened by surrounding forces of other religious ideals, as well as political forces such as worship of the emperor. By affirming the apostolic leadership of the Catholic Church, the church fathers vindicated the mission of Christians to give themselves wholeheartedly to the gospel and to defend the gospel against heretics. Thus, while the word *catholic* literally meant an active process of making whole, it took on the meaning of universal orthodoxy as the early church assumed an apologetic position in the empire due to religious, political, and cultural forces threatening it. Hence, the birth of the Catholic Church in the first few centuries after the death of Jesus involved the mission to preach the gospel to all parts of the world as the revelation of God's truth and love in history, for the sake of unity in the face of divisions.

WAS JESUS CATHOLIC?

Today the Catholic Church is known as the universal church, but what exactly do we mean by universal and is this understanding of catholic faithful to the message of Jesus? If we are to draw a connection between the word *catholic* and the mission of Jesus, we would have to rely on its root meaning, "according to the whole," for what Jesus preached was not a church defending itself in the face of opposition but the in-breaking reign of God. Based on what we know from the Gospels we can make several inferences: Jesus was not a "catholic" but a Jew, and the reign of God preached by Jesus was not a universal concept to be mandated but a change in lifestyle and direction. The central message of Jesus, the reign of God, is a new, dynamic way of being in the world. The reign of God is a subtle and powerful reality, far more dynamic than any kind of realm we can conceive. Mark Hathaway and Leonardo Boff write that the actual word Jesus used in Aramaic to speak of God's reign—*malkuta*—is "much more similar to the concept of the Tao or to the Buddhist Dharma than to any kind of kingdom we might imagine." "The word's roots," they write, "elicit the image of a fruitful arm poised to create, or a coiled spring that is ready to unwind with all the verdant potential of the earth." *Malkuta* connotes an "empowering vision based on the divine presence in the cosmos, liberating and empowering a process toward communion, differentiation and interiority."[9] What broke through in the person of Jesus was a new consciousness and relatedness to God that ushered in the world a new way of being God-centered, earth-centered, and in communion with one another.

Walter Ong suggests that the word *catholic* was adopted by the church because it described Jesus' parable about the reign of God, which he likened to yeast that "a woman took and kneaded into three measures of flour. Eventually the whole mass of dough began to rise."[10] Although making bread is domestic work associated with women, we should not overlook the connection between the reign of God preached by Jesus and women, indicating that the reign of God is not an abstract concept; rather, we might say, it is household work. Anyone who has worked with yeast and flour knows that making bread is a careful process; kneading the dough is an art that calls for patience, perseverance, and attentiveness to the shape of the dough as the yeast is worked through it. The yeast must permeate throughout the dough if the bread is to rise consistently. In a similar way, "the kingdom or the church is a limitless, growing reality, destined ultimately to be present everywhere and to affect everything, though by no means to convert everything into itself." The reign of God belongs to those who are willing to work with their hands, heads and hearts for the good of the whole. "Yeast acts on dough but it does not convert all the dough into yeast, nor is it able to do so or meant to do so."[11]

In light of this parable the word *catholic* does not mean a universal presence absorbing everything into itself but an active growing, spreading, or acting upon so as to transform, rising from the old into a new unity. Jesus, in a sense, was like the woman kneading the dough; he persistently acted upon the lure of the Spirit to preach the new reign of God, going from town to town and village to village—not forcing his message upon anyone but inviting others to listen, be attentive, to trust in God, and to change their ways. The reign of God preached by Jesus meant a new consciousness of being in the world, a consciousness of relatedness, inclusivity, non-duality, and community. Jesus ushered in a new presence of God, a new realm of God based on the empowerment of community. His message was like yeast permeating the hearts of his listeners, calling for a redirection of being in the world, a new way of relating in the human community, and a new connection between heaven and earth. His radical message required conversion, change of heart, and commitment; once the hand was put to the plow, one was not to look back but to go forward, because this new reign was breaking in from the future, that is, the realm of possibilities held open by a new consciousness of God's presence.[12]

The good news that emerged in the life of Jesus was the news of God's healing love; the binding of wounds; the reconciling of relationships torn apart by anger, hurt, jealousy, or vengeance; the revelation that love is stronger than death and that forgiveness is the act of love that creates a new future. Jesus the Christ shows us what is possible for humanity. In Jesus is seen, in the context of the whole complex of events in which he participated, what God intends for all human beings. He represents the consummation of the evolutionary creative process that God has been effecting in and through the world.[13]

THE DYNAMIC OF WHOLE-MAKING

Jesus' catholicity, if we can use such a term, was shown in the way he brought people together—physically, emotionally, and spiritually—and healed them of their divisions. He preached oneness of mind and heart centered in God, and he spoke of the reign of God as a dynamic process of relatedness by which the world could move forward to a new level of unity, ultimately so that all could be one in God. Jesus made things whole, and the Gospels are replete with stories of Jesus' "whole-making." His public mission of whole-making began in the Temple, where he opened the scroll to read from the prophet Isaiah:

> When he came to Nazareth, where he had been brought up, he went to the synagogue on the sabbath day, as was his custom. He stood up to read, and the scroll of the prophet Isaiah was given to him. He unrolled the scroll and found the place where it was written: "The Spirit of the Lord is upon me, because he has anointed me to bring good news to the poor. He has sent me to proclaim release to the captives and recovery of sight to the blind, to let the oppressed go free, to proclaim the year of the Lord's favor." And he rolled up the scroll, gave it back to the attendant, and sat down. The eyes of all in the synagogue were fixed on him. Then he began to say to them, "Today this scripture has been fulfilled in your hearing." (Lk 4:16-21)

As Jesus announced his mission of whole-making, he directed himself to those who are in need of being made whole: the brokenhearted, captives, those in darkness, prisoners, those who are grieving, the poor, the blind, and the oppressed. He indicated that his mission is not one of power but one of healing, making whole through the "the Spirit of the Lord," the Spirit who anointed Jesus to reach out to those who are broken or disconnected from the fullness of life. Jesus made whole the lepers who were imprisoned by their debilitating disease and rejected by society, the blind man whose blindness was attributed to the sins of his parents, the broken hearts of Mary and Martha upon learning of their brother's death. The author of Matthew's gospel writes of Jesus' mission:

"The blind receive their sight, the lame walk, the lepers are cleansed, the deaf hear, and the dead are raised, and the poor have good news brought to them" (Mt 11:5). To make whole for Jesus was to heal physical, emotional, and spiritual divisions—to save. Through his relationships with women, the poor, lepers, Sadducees, tax collectors, and others marginalized or shunned by society, Jesus showed that whole-making is salvific. Salvation is not an abstract universal; rather, it is concrete and personal and is expressed in reconciliation and renewed relationships. Dietrich Bonhoeffer wrote that our relationship to God is not a "religious" relationship to the highest, most powerful, and best Being imaginable; rather, our relation to God is a new life in "existence for others," through participation in the being of Jesus.[14] In Latin the word *salus* ("salvation") means "health." To be "saved" is to be restored to health, to be made whole. To be made healthy one has to recognize one's need to be made whole. Jesus said: "Those who are well have no need of a physician, but those who are sick" (Mt 9:12). Jesus did not force salvation but elicited it from others as a desire. When Jesus approached the blind man, for example, he asked, "What do you want me to do for you?" The man answered, "'Lord, let me see again.' Jesus said to him, 'Receive your sight; your faith has saved you.' Immediately he regained his sight and followed him, glorifying God; and all the people, when they saw it, praised God" (Lk 18:41–43). What Jesus indicates here is that the glory begins with desire for wholeness and appears in those who are made healthy and whole.

Jesus' dynamic process of whole-making was not imposed but was offered in response to needs based on relationships of mutuality, dialogue, and openness. Jesus sought to create wholes where there were divisions—whole people, whole communities, wholesome living—for the glory of God. The Greek word for sin, *hamartia*, means "to miss the mark." When we sin, we miss the mark or we live out of focus, promoting "dis-ease" in the cosmos; relationships are broken, violence ensues, and we become disconnected from one another and from the earth. The health we seek requires concrete relationships of compassion, peace, and forgiveness; it requires attentiveness to people, earth, sun, moon, and stars, seeing within each created being the divine goodness, beauty, and wisdom. A healthy cosmos requires healthy people who live in openness, compassionate love, and receptivity to others, accepting others as part of self because we are one in the depth of God's love.

Whole-making is a process of engagement, and being made whole empowers others to be made whole as well. Jesus preached a healthy life for a healthy creation. The ten lepers who were cured of their disease, for example, were to go forth with deeper faith (Lk 17:11–19); Mary's mourning at the tomb turned to joy at the sight of the Lord, but she was not to cling to her experience of Jesus (Jn 20:1, 17). She was to go forth and tell others the good news. Jesus' reign of God as whole-making has within it a dynamism of movement, of going forth in new relatedness to the world, to engage others by drawing into unity those who are apart and to heal those who are divided. Those who follow Jesus are to be healthy and to help make the whole creation healthy as well. The life of Jesus is the emergence of catholicity in cosmic evolution.

WHOLE-MAKING AND COSTLY LOVE

If the reign of God is based on whole-making or drawing unity out of multiplicity, then we can say the ultimate act of whole-making, which becomes paradigmatic of Christian discipleship, is Jesus' suffering and death on the cross. The death of Jesus shows the type of engagement that makes whole-making a forward movement in the cosmos. Whereas the Greeks believed that unity could be achieved only by transcending the material world and being absorbed into the undifferentiated oneness of the Godhead, Jesus showed that unity is achieved by reconciling separate bodies into a unified whole. According to Hellenic thought, commitment to the One or unity with God meant an erasure of difference, since the body was to be transcended or denied in the pursuit of spiritual perfection. In *Exclusion and Embrace* Miroslav Volf writes that the "One" in whom Paul seeks to locate the unity of all humanity is not disincarnate transcendence but the crucified and resurrected Jesus Christ. The "principle" of unity has a name, and the name designates a person with a body that has suffered on the cross. All are made one body of God's children without regard to gender or race because of the cross (cf. Gal 3:28). Paul writes: "Because there is one bread we who are many are one body, for we all partake of the one bread" (1 Cor 10:17). The "bread" that Paul refers to is the crucified body of Christ, the body that has refused to remain a self-enclosed singularity, but has opened itself up so that others can freely partake of it. Volf explains: "The grounding of unity and universality in the scandalous particularity of the suffering body of God's Messiah is what makes Paul's thought so profoundly different from the kinds of beliefs in the all-importance of the undifferentiated universal spirit that would make one 'ashamed of being in the body.'"[15] Far from being one *against* the many, the significance of Christ crucified is the self-giving of the one *for* the many. The crucified Messiah creates unity by giving himself. Because Christ unites different bodies into one body through his suffering on the cross, it is the surrender of the crucified One through self-giving love that is the basis of Christian community. The power of love that makes whole is the Spirit. It is the Spirit sent by Christ who conforms us to Christ, not by erasing our identity, but by shaping the persons we are into the vessels of love we are created to be. The Spirit sets us free because the Spirit leads us to the truth of who we are in God. Thus, the gospel is a constant call to freedom, to shape our own lives rather than allow ourselves to be influenced by an imaginary world order or to have any code simply thrust upon us.[16]

To follow Christ is to be engaged in such a way that one's stance of being in the world is unitive not divisive. Eucharistic life sacramentalizes the vocation of whole-making by offering one's life for the sake of drawing together that which is divided. Eucharist is being bread broken and eaten for the hungry of the world.[17] It is the food that gives strength to make every stranger beloved, the "yes" of our lives to God's mysterious cruciform love. Volf writes:

> We would most profoundly misunderstand the Eucharist if we thought of it only as a sacrament of God's embrace of which we are the fortunate beneficiaries. Inscribed in the very heart of God's grace is the rule that we can be its recipients only if we do not resist being made into its agents. What happens to us must be done by us.[18]

The cross is not merely Christ's passion, Volf writes, but it is God's passion. It reveals the total self-giving love of God that reaches out to estranged humanity and embraces every stranger as the beloved.[19] In the cross we are embraced by the Trinity of love, who loves us with the same love with which the persons of the Trinity love one another. The crucified Christ signifies a space in God's self for the other and an invitation for the enemy to come in.[20] In the cross, therefore, we are taken up in the eternal embrace of the triune God of love.[21] This embrace in love by the crucified Christ in which the arms of Christ are the arms of the triune God is, according to Volf, the meaning of Eucharist. "The eucharist," he writes, "is the ritual time in which we celebrate this divine 'making-space-for-us-and-inviting-us-in.'" However, it is not simply being embraced by God but an empowering of God's love by which we are to embrace others, including our enemies. That is, "having been embraced by God, we must make space for others in ourselves and invite them in—even our enemies."[22]

Understanding the Eucharist as the internalization of God's love leads to the centrality of the Eucharist as the basis of catholic life. The truly catholic personality, according to Orthodox theologian John Zizioulas, is one centered around the mystery of the Eucharist. In receiving the Eucharist each person receives the whole Christ—head and members—so that the entire body is present in each member.[23] In this way each person who partakes of the Eucharist is made into an ecclesial person, and all persons are internal to the very being of one another. The Eucharist, therefore, signifies that each member is not external to the other members but rather internally related to the other members of the body of Christ. Our relationship to Christ is our relationship to one another. If we say yes to the embrace of the crucified Christ, then we must be willing to offer that embrace to our neighbor, our brother or sister, whoever he or she might be, for the person we willingly embrace has already been embraced by Christ. The Eucharist, therefore, is the sacrament of evolution because every act of Eucharist is an act of making a new future through a new divine presence, a new relatedness, a new freedom to love. But this eucharistic embrace as an act of whole-making means letting go and receiving the other into oneself.[24] It requires death to the old self that refuses to embrace another and openness to the other as part of oneself. Whole-making is the desire to be part of a greater whole, and Eucharist sacramentalizes the whole.

If the life of Jesus sets the pattern of whole-making, which includes reconciliation, forgiveness, peacemaking, and compassion, and if this pattern permeates the mass of creation—humanity and cosmos—then we would have to say that catholic appears wherever there is movement toward overcoming differences and making wholes. That is, one does not have to be baptized in the Catholic Church to be a whole-maker; rather, one must have the desire for wholeness and a willingness to help create it. Such a person is catholic in the broadest sense. The cross is the ultimate making whole by which everyone can participate. It is the act of self-gift that makes a unified whole, which neither love nor suffering could do alone. Jesus' whole-making is self-surrender for a greater good, and anyone who makes whole by self-surrender for a greater good is following Jesus, whether or not they are conscious of doing so.

A CATHOLIC UNIVERSE?

If we understand *catholic* as a dynamic process of making whole, then *catholicity*, at its roots, is participation in creating greater unity through deepening relationships; catholic describes the whole evolutionary universe. From the Big Bang onward, creation is endowed with an inner dynamic toward wholeness because it is itself wholeness in movement. Whole-making appears in a human person in such a way that evolution is given its meaning and purpose—to make whole by creatively bringing together what is divided or apart. Jesus admonished his disciples not to cling to him, not to covet what they had seen, but to go out to the world and to draw together what is apart—to forgive, make peace, reconcile, show mercy, in short, to continue making wholes where there are divisions, for this is the meaning of Christ and all those who follow Christ. Hence, I suggest that *catholic* and *Christ* are two words that stand for wholeness and unity. Catholicity is dynamic engagement in whole-making, and Christ is the emergent wholeness of divine love that erupts in Jesus of Nazareth. To be catholic is to be donative, to be self-giving love by which the Spirit of love weaves together the fragments of life into evolutive wholes. The true catholic, therefore, emerges where the Spirit dynamically weaves the oneness of God.

Evolution means that Christ is not yet complete and we are not complete. In Jesus, God's self-communication to creation explodes into history. Evolution assumes an explicit direction. God evolves the universe and brings it to its completion through the instrumentality of human beings. Jesus is the Christ, the climax of that long development whereby the world becomes aware of itself and comes into the direct presence of God.[25] The teaching that Jesus is the Christ means Jesus is not any person but *the* fully integrated person in whom God has revealed Godself in the most complete way.[26] In Jesus, the Christ becomes explicit; hence, the meaning of the cosmos becomes explicit as well. The whole creation is intended to be a unity in love in union with God. Those who proclaim themselves Christian proclaim belief in the risen Christ and must be on the way toward development of a transcultural consciousness and thus transcultural encounters. In Jesus we see that the future of the material universe is linked to the fulfillment of the community of human beings in whom the world has come to consciousness.[27] The evolutionary process is moving toward evolution of consciousness and ultimately toward evolution of spirit, from the birth of mind to the birth of the whole Christ.[28]

What took place in the life of Jesus must take place in our lives as well, if creation is to move toward completion and transformation in God. Healing divisions and forming relationships that promote greater unity are sources of God's gracious presence emerging from within the history of the cosmos. Jesus marks a new direction in evolution toward integrated being, healthy relationships, and healing presence, all of which contribute to the act of a new future. As the wellspring of divine love emerging from within, Jesus shows us what it means to be a human person and the way to deepen our humanity toward the fullness of life. His disciples recognized him as the Christ, the anointed One (Mk 8:27), the One who will bring about a new future, a new creation, and who has already done so in our present age. The Christ emerges in Jesus, and the humanity of Jesus shows us what the Christ looks like; his humanity is our humanity, and his life is our life. What took place in Jesus' life must take place in ours as well if the fullness of Christ is to come to be. "Our salvation is necessary for the completion of Christ," wrote the Cistercian Isaac of Stella.[29] Christ is the future of this evolutionary cosmos, the One who trinitizes creation into a household of unity, the integrated unified center of persons in love. There is no birth of Christ, however, without the Spirit. It is the Creator Spirit who continues to breathe new life in evolutionary creation, who weaves together the cosmic body of Christ. The Spirit is the "holon maker," the One who breathes new life, generates new love, searches for a new future by uniting what is separate or apart, by healing and making whole. Where there is the Spirit, there is the divine Word expressed in the rich variety of creation, and where there is the Spirit and Word there is the fountain fullness of love. Christ symbolizes this unity of love; hence, the fullness of Christ is the creative diversity of all that exists held together by the Spirit of luminous love.

Chapter Five

Resurrection and Transformation

EMPOWERED NEW LIFE

Christianity is based on several core beliefs that are shocking. One is that God becomes a human person, a carpenter turned preacher. The other is that a dead man is raised to new life. As fantastic as these claims are, the whole of Christianity rests on the death and resurrection of Jesus Christ. Saint Paul wrote, "If Christ has not been raised from the dead, our preaching is useless and so is your faith" (1 Cor 15:17). Without the resurrection of Jesus from the dead we Christians are indeed foolish people, following a man who died as a criminal. Despite the fact that Easter is the central Christian message, most people are less energized by Easter than by Christmas. It is much easier to rejoice in the birth of an infant than in a dead man rising from the grave. But without Easter, Christmas is undone. Easter is the core of Christian faith.

There are problems, however. For one, we celebrate Easter as the victory over sin. "O Happy Fault!" we proclaim, "for if Adam had not sinned, Christ would not have come." Should we not be celebrating the power of God's humble love instead of sin, a love so great that even death cannot vanquish it? Second, most Christians believe that Jesus went to a place called heaven and will come again to judge the living and the dead. But how do we make sense of heaven in an evolutionary world? What does resurrection from the dead mean in a universe that will continue for about 100 trillion more years?

The earliest account of resurrection in the letter to the Corinthians points to fulfillment. Jesus Christ ushers in the new creation through his death and resurrection; he shows what is intended for the world, a new way of being human, with healthy relationships for the whole cosmos—new life, new bodies for a new cosmos. As N. T. Wright notes, the portrait of Jesus in the resurrection narratives ought to surprise us in two respects. First, Jesus is never depicted as a heavenly being, radiant with glory. He does not appear in brilliant light or otherworldly. He appears in the narratives as a human being among human beings, walking along the road to Emmaus or eating fish. Second, these appearances of Jesus are almost routinely depicted as bodily appearances; some close friends did not recognize him and others did (see Jn 21:12). Wright states: "The picture of Jesus in the canonical gospels is of one who is embodied as a full human being, but whose body has in some way been transformed, so that it now possesses new and striking, not to say startling, properties."[1] The Gospels, in effect, describe more or less what Paul states in his theoretical framework. The resurrection of Jesus from the dead is an event involving neither the resuscitation nor the abandonment of a physical body. It is a transformation into a new mode of physicality, an event for which there was no precedent and of which there remains as yet no subsequent example.

Belief in the resurrection empowered early Christians. "The resurrection of Jesus . . . is not an absurd event but the symbol and starting point of the new world," ushering in "not simply a new religious possibility or a new ethic but a new creation."[2] This wholehearted belief in the risen Christ inspired Christians to risk their lives for the sake of the gospel, sometimes enduring brutal physical martyrdom, such as that mentioned in the accounts of the deaths of Ignatius of Antioch; Polycarp, the Bishop of Smyrna; and the young women Perpetua and Felicity. Dominic Crossan claimed that early Christians believed God had called them to work with him, in the power of the Spirit; the bodily resurrection of Jesus is about the justice of God.[3] Crossan states that the resurrection is about "cosmic transformation of this world from a world of evil and injustice and impurity and violence into a world of justice and peace and purity and holiness."[4] Wright says: "If Jesus, the Messiah, was the End in person, God's-future-arrived-in-the-present, then those who belonged to Jesus and followed him and were empowered by his Spirit were charged with transforming the present, as far as they were able, in light of that future."[5] The early Christians looked back to the Christ event with joy and looked forward to an event yet to come, begun at Easter and yet to be completed. The writings of Paul clearly point to new life in Christ, a transformation of our present bodily life into a new, glorious bodily (Eph 1:19–20) existence that means a transformation of the whole earthly cosmos itself (1 Cor 15:28).

Wright states that the meaning of resurrection changed in the late second century, when people started using the term *resurrection* to mean something different from what it meant in Judaism and early Christianity. As Christianity eventually became a formalized state religion, removed in time from the historical event of Jesus, resurrection became a spiritual experience, "a disembodied hope in the future."[6] The influence of Platonic metaphysics on the shape of Christian spirituality cannot be overstated. Greek Christian writers like Origen of Alexandria and Justin Martyr adopted the Platonic distinctions of soul, spirit, and body, which led to an emphasis of soul over body and the notion of eternal life as a purely spiritual experience. The difficulty of translating Jewish ideas into Greek compounded the problem of the resurrection. The Jews believed that the world of space, time, and matter was flawed but good and that God would bless the good with a final, physical resurrection. But Greek-speaking Christians influenced by Plato saw our cosmos as weak, mutable, and fallen. The idea was not to make it right but to escape it and leave behind our material bodies. Belief in the resurrection entered the modern period wrapped in a Platonic, spiritualized understanding of heaven, and the cosmic and risen Christ became a ghostlike principle. Wright states:

> The idea of the human Jesus now being in heaven, in his thoroughly embodied risen state, comes as a shock to many people, including many Christians. Sometimes this is because many people think that Jesus, having been divine, stopped being divine and became human, and then, having been human for a while, stopped being human and went back to being divine.[7]

Wright's work on the resurrection together with other New Testament studies, makes clear the meaning of resurrection: bodily life is not valueless because it will die. Rather, God will raise it to new life that will last into God's future. The ascension of Jesus means that the human Jesus is with us as Lord, the hope of what we and all creation aim for; heaven is created life transformed in God.[8] Heaven is not a place of non-materiality. It begins in this earthly life as we cooperate with God to change our weak, frail, and incomplete human lives into vessels of God's transforming love. Our culture is so familiar with the Platonic idea that heaven is a purely spiritual place that the idea of a solid body being not only present but also thoroughly at home there seems like a mistake. Heaven is the reality of God's indwelling presence, God's light and love, as Saint Francis of Assisi described it.[9] It is the space in God where suffering is transformed by love and evil is overcome by goodness. Heaven is not a place of disembodied spirits but an embrace of love that transforms this present earthly life with its frailties and weaknesses into the divine presence of enduring love. It is earth's openness to God, the "space of the possible."[10] "When the New Testament speaks of God's kingdom it never, ever, refers to heaven pure and simple. It always refers to God's kingdom coming *on earth as in heaven*, as Jesus himself taught us to pray. . . . We have been used to seeing 'heaven' as a place separated from earth, somewhere far away."[11] But earth is not a training ground for heaven. It is, rather, the very place where heaven unfolds. Even Saint Francis of Assisi knew that heaven is not a place above earth but God's indwelling love that enlightens and inflames, opening up one's vision to the truth of this world in God. Heaven, therefore, is not another world but this world clearly seen.

RESURRECTION AND EVOLUTION

If resurrection means new life, empowered by the Holy Spirit, a new future of embodied existence, how do we understand this new life in the context of evolution? In his April 15, 2006, Easter Vigil homily, Pope Benedict XVI described the resurrection of Jesus as "a qualitative leap in the history of 'evolution' and of life in general toward a new future life":

> The Resurrection was like an explosion of light, an explosion of love which dissolved the hitherto indissoluble compenetration of "dying and becoming." It ushered in a new dimension of being, a new dimension of life in which,

in a transformed way, matter too was integrated and through which a new world emerges. It is clear that this event is not just some miracle from the past, the occurrence of which could be ultimately a matter of indifference to us. It is a qualitative leap in the history of "evolution" and of life in general toward a new future life, toward a new world which, starting from Christ, already continuously permeates this world of ours, transforms it and draws it to itself.

The pope's densely packed message points to the essence of the resurrection: new life and a new future for the cosmos, which is our home. It is not an otherworldly miracle but a "this worldly" trans-formation, an "explosion of light," a new Big Bang that launches a new creation and hence a new relationship to God. Benedict states that the resurrection "ushered in a new dimension of being, a new dimension of life in which, in a transformed way, matter too was integrated and through which a new world emerges." What the pope indicates is that transformation is integral to resurrection. In this mysterious event of Jesus Christ, something new happens, but not in a miraculous way, as if God suspended the laws of nature to raise Jesus from the dead. Rather, the resurrection is about the trans-formation of creaturely life from within, because creaturely life is God's own self-communicative life. Karl Rahner said that "God creates in order to give God's self to creation as its final fulfill-ment." Rahner saw the Christ event as "the irreversible beginning of God's self-giving to creation that will find its fulfillment only when the whole of creation is transformed in Christ."[12] The Franciscan theologian Bonaventure envisioned the whole cosmos transformed in Christ when he wrote:

> All things are said to be transformed in the transfiguration of Christ, in as far as something of each creature was transfig-ured in Christ. For as a human being, Christ has something in common with all creatures. With the stone he shares exist-ence; with plants he shares life; with animals he shares sensa-tion; and the angels he shares intelligence. Therefore, all things are said to be transformed in Christ since—in his hu-man nature—he embraces something of every creature in him-self when he is transfigured.[13]

It is because creation emerges from within the divine implicate order that the existence of creatures is transcendent by nature because God is ever new. The whole creation is, in a sense, resurrection from the beginning. Evolution as God's creative act is the active self-transcendence toward new life. Creation flows out of the dynamic, self-communicative love of God and, like God, goes forth in dynamic relationships toward greater unity in love. The resurrection recapitulates the whole evolutionary emergent creation as a forward movement to become something new, a new reign of God, a new heaven on earth. What took place in Jesus Christ is intended for the whole cosmos, union and transformation in the divine embrace of love.

TRANSCENDENT IN LOVE

The events of Jesus' life based on the gospel narratives show us that resurrection is the culmination of the Christ event and hence recapitulates the whole cosmos: suffering and death anticipate new life. Could God have brought about new life in the cosmos without Jesus' suffering and death? Could Jesus have wrought salvation by living to old age and dying peacefully in his sleep? Of course God could have done so, because with God all things are possible. Such an answer, however, fails to accept fully the integral relationship between God and creation. Death is not merely a surd, an unfortunate product of creation. Rather, death is integral to who God is—self-giving love. The giving up and handing over of oneself is the generation of new life; the self-emptying of the Father is the life of the Son. Without death there is no fullness of life; hence, death is integral to life. The whole Christian message based on death is simply this: without death there is no new life. Everything living dies, and everything that dies lives. In the world of nature evolution is contingent on death. Because of death the natural world sustains new life, even in the face of massive extinctions. On the human level, however, death becomes an affliction, an obstacle, and a curse due to sin; the very resistance to death becomes the power of death over life. When we say "by death Christ has conquered death," we profess the reality of death as the necessary event for greater life.

We can see the relationship between death and life in the cosmic story. The fourteen billion of years of evolutionary history have been made possible because of death in the universe. Judy Cannato writes, "The giving over of life on behalf of ever-expanding creativity is integral to life itself. The massive star that was mother to our Sun met with fiery death, her form completely annihilated by the explosive force of the blast. And yet she exists in each of us, in the cells of our bodies that are composed of her dust."[14] Death is what makes life possible; it is necessary to the evolution of life because it is the letting go of isolated existence for the sake of greater union. Holmes Rolston describes nature as "cruciform." There is struggle throughout nature for survival, and one might see in nature the capacity for suffering to evolve. Yet this struggle in nature includes a struggle resulting in more diverse and more complex forms of life. Rolston writes:

> This whole evolutionary upslope is a calling in which renewed life comes by blasting the old. Life is gathered up in the midst of its throes, a blessed tragedy, lived in grace through a besetting storm. . . . The cruciform creation is, in the end, deiform, godly, just because of this element of struggle, not in spite of it. There is a great divine 'yes' hidden behind and within every 'no' of crushing nature. . . . Long before humans arrived, the way of nature was already a *via dolorosa*. In that sense, the aura of the cross is cast backward across the whole global story, and it forever outlines the future.[15]

Rolston points out that suffering is not absurd to nature; rather, it is a key to the whole transformative principle of nature. Suffering makes nature wild and unpredictable, and yet out of this wildness comes amazing beauty and wondrous new creation. In *Pilgrim at Tinker Creek* Annie Dillard writes: "The whole creation is one lunatic fringe . . . no claims of any and all revelation could be so farfetched as a single giraffe."[16] It is wild, unpredictable, and seemingly illogical nature that gives birth to us humans. Yet we humans want to control this wild nature that is our home. We want to manipulate it through technology and contain its wildness so that we can control suffering and limit pain, aiming for some sort of artificial happiness. As much as we want to avoid suffering and death, with its inner conflict and darkness, we are afraid to change because we fear what new life may mean. Dillard writes:

> It is the fixed that horrifies us, the fixed that assails us with the tremendous force of its mindlessness. The fixed is a Mason jar, and we can't beat it open. . . . The fixed is the world without fire—dead flint, dead timber, and nowhere a spark. It is motion without direction, force without power, the aimless procession of caterpillars round the rim of a vase, and I hate it because at any moment I myself might step to that charmed and glistening thread.[17]

The fear of death underscores some of the trends in information technology today. The rise of apocalyptic artificial intelligence is a desire for cyber immortality, overcoming the limits of suffering and death through artificial means. However, suffering and death reflect life's contingencies and inherent spontaneity. When the artificiality of a random-number algorithm replaces the surprises of natural richness, we lose something of human life: the sense of what it means to be created, dependent, contingent, and finite. Alfred Kracher writes, "A planet ruled by predictability where all contingency is eliminated is also a planet dominated by unchecked evil."[18] Harmony requires wildness—the unpredictability of nature, the contingency that makes the world what it is—a sense of astonishment, wonder, and awe.[19] Death is the harmony of our wild, created nature with the wild love of God.

RELEASE INTO WHOLENESS

If death is the basis of new resurrected life, what exactly is death in a cosmos where matter and energy are convertible, as Einstein discovered? Does matter really die, that is, does matter become extinct and disappear when the breath of life terminates? Or is death the release of physical form into the unbroken wholeness of life in the universe? One could hold to the dissolution of matter at death if one believed that matter and spirit are separate entities, so that in death the spirit ceases to be vivifying and matter disappears. But such an idea violates the present understanding of matter and energy, in which all matter is energy and all energy is matter. Death, I suggest, is not the dissolution of matter but the transformation of matter into energy and hence into memory or information in the universe. If death were truly an absolute termination of life, then the cosmos would hold no memory. Death as the transformation of matter into energy is the source of memory in the universe, and hence the energy that contains information for the renewal of life. Because of death, transcendence and new life are possible.

Pierre Teilhard de Chardin believed that the presence of pain, suffering, and death is not just structurally logical in an evolving universe but statistically necessary because matter is primarily multiple and unorganized. Through the evolutionary processes in which God is immanent, the multiple is unified and organized, converging gradually toward unity in God. Therefore, Teilhard suggests, "if to create is to unite (evolutively, gradually), then God cannot create without evil appearing as a shadow."[20] Teilhard states that pain, suffering, and death in an evolving universe are woven into the creative process itself. They are not solely experiences that sentient beings inflict upon one another by necessity or by choice. Rather, they are inherent aspects of a universe in the process of unification and transformation toward God. He writes:

> By virtue of the very structure of the nothingness over which God leans, in order to create he can proceed in only one way. He must under his attractive influence arrange and unify little by little. . . . But what is the inevitable counterpart of the complete success which is obtained by following a process of this type? Is it not the payment of a certain amount of waste? It involves disharmony or physical decomposition in the pre-living, suffering in the living, and sin in the domain of liberty.[21]

For Teilhard, creation "cannot progress toward unity without giving rise to . . . some evil here or there and that by statistical necessity."[22] Hence, writes Gloria Schwab, "so long as disorder, disunity, and disorganization endure within the creative movement toward God, Teilhard suggests, so long do pain, suffering, and death endure as inherent, inescapable elements of the process."[23]

MATTER AND SPIRIT

The death and resurrection of Jesus make sense as the power of God's love when we see love as the source of the cosmos and the transcendent nature of created reality. If the life of Jesus is exemplary for all life in the cosmos, then what we say about Jesus must be true for all life in the cosmos. The problem of the resurrection, of course, follows the incredible belief that the body rises from the dead. Since the human body changes throughout earthly life, from birth to death, which body will a human being possess at the moment of resurrection? Saint Paul talks about a "spiritual body" rather than a resuscitated corpse (1 Cor 15:44) but what is a spiritual body? What is the body of the risen Christ? What about the bodies of all those who have died over the millennia? Are they in heaven, or are they asleep in their graves? Will they rise from their graves at the second coming of Christ? These are the questions that plague both believers and nonbelievers, primarily because the idea of rising from the dead seems so absurd. But—as Saint Paul reminds us—if Jesus is not raised from the dead then our faith in Christ is useless (1 Cor 15:14). Understanding the resurrection in a new, life-giving way is one of the most important tasks of theology today.

The problem of the resurrection has been compounded by the adoption of Plato's primacy of the spirit over matter and Descartes' absolutizing of this dualism. Commenting on his famous dictum, "I think therefore I am," Descartes wrote, "The soul by which I am what I am is entirely distinct from body, and is even more easy to know than is the latter; and even if body were not, the soul would not cease to be what it is."[24] Following this line of dualism we say, as Pope Pius XII did in *Humani Generis*, "the body may come about through biological evolution but the soul is created immediately by God" (no. 36). Or we pray that "the souls of the faithful departed rest in peace." Although the doctrine of evolution affirms the unfolding of energized matter—and not spirit *and* matter— many people have a difficult time accepting the fact that creation, including the human person, is always one in relation to God.

Quantum physics has taught us that what we think of as matter is actually interconnected webs of energy. The discovery of relativity and the mysterious nature of matter and energy have led

scientists to conclude that matter is not composed of basic building blocks but of complicated webs of relations. The interconnectedness of life in the universe means that we are part of the
intrinsic value of all living beings; the human person is one particular strand in the web of life. Integral systems tell us that this universe is thoroughly interconnected, so that even our own being is
not our own. Reality by its very nature is interconnectedness. Heidi
Russell writes:

> If the so-called particles out of which we are made are in fact
> not particles but manifestations of fields of energy, quanta or
> little packets of energy, if you will, then this thing we call a
> body is not a thing at all! There is a falsity to the concept of
> object, matter, or body. There is really no such thing as par-
> ticles or objects or matter, but rather only space and energy.
> What we call the material world is not matter at all, but rather
> occasions or processes.[25]

If there is no such thing as materialism then what we call a body
needs to be reconsidered. Maybe as Russell points out "embodi-
ment is the collection of previous occasions, processes, and events
that shape the probability waves of the future."[26] If matter is not
brute matter devoid of spirit or energy, then we need not conceive
of the body as a thing so much as the actualization of who we are
that is shaped by who and what we are related to. The notion of the
body as the actualization of interrelatedness also puts new light on
the soul. Mark Graves states that the soul is not a substance but "a
constellation of constitutive relationships that enable real possibility in a human person."[27] Thus new realities of body and soul make
up the human person, not as distinct essences but as interrelated
fields of energy that include the mind. Whereas in the past we
thought the mind was something separate and distinct from the
body, many scholars now believe that the mind is in the body and
the body is in the mind. The work of neurologist Antonio D'Amasio,
for example, shows that "the body may constitute the indispensable frame for the neural processes that we experience as mind
. . . that the mind had to be first about the body, or it could not
have been."[28] The mind, like the body, is more like a complex
energy field or a complexity of fields rather than an inert substance or entity. Rupert Sheldrake writes that "fields cannot be

explained in terms of matter; rather matter is explained in terms of the energy within fields."[29] Physics and biology today indicate that interrelated fields form the stuff of matter rather than matter forming fields.

Mathematician and philosopher Alfred North Whitehead sought to develop an understanding of the God-world relationship based on contemporary insights of science. According to William Hasker, Whitehead believed that mind and body are then not two different realities, as Descartes proposed following the lead of Plato.[30] Nor are they to be understood as form and matter as Aquinas suggested following the lead of Aristotle.[31] As Whitehead writes, "they are two dialectically related dimensions of one and the same physical reality at all levels of existence and activity within Nature."[32] Following Whitehead, Bracken suggests three ways the mind expresses the spirit:

> The human body as a material reality is not opposed to the reality of spirit, but is its necessary self-expression or self-manifestation. Secondly, the way in which the body is the self-expression of mind or spirit is to exist from moment to moment as a complex structured field of activity for all the "decisions" made by the actual occasions contained within it. Thirdly, this limited field of activity for a single bodily reality is continually being incorporated first into the much larger field of activity proper to its natural environment (ultimately creation as a whole) and then into the unlimited field of activity proper to God as divine Spirit. In this way, the body as a finite field of activity is from moment to moment incorporated into the field of activity proper to God and thereby achieves at every moment objective immortality within God.[33]

According to Bracken, nature is composed of hierarchical ordered fields of activity dynamically interacting at different levels of existence.[34] What we call matter and spirit are a "combination of energy content and organizational patterns incorporated into structured fields of activity out of which actual occasions originate."[35] In *Process and Reality* Whitehead writes, "In the philosophy of organism it is not 'substance' which is permanent, but 'form.'"[36] Thus what we call matter and spirit are really organizational patterns and energy. As Teilhard de Chardin postulated, physical reality is composed of two dynamically interrelated dimensions or parts, or what he called "withinness" and "withoutness." The *within* is the mental aspect and the *without* is the physical aspect of the same stuff. The relationship between withinness and withoutness points to the role of consciousness at the heart of matter.[37] Joseph Bracken writes: "Together they (matter and energy) constitute and evolve as a single nondual psychophysical reality. Neither 'spirit' nor 'matter' can exist without the other."[38] If matter is the form or pattern of structured fields of activity, then spirit is the interrelated energy of the events taking place in the field of activity.

This new understanding of matter and spirit relates to a new understanding of God. Bracken states that in Whiteheadian terms, the Trinity of divine persons is "a personally ordered society of actual occasions presiding over a completely unlimited field of activity."[39] The trinitarian God, Bracken states, can be understood as "three divine subjects of experience who together co-constitute an all-encompassing field of activity structured by their ongoing relationality to one another. This divine field of activity or divine matrix serves as the origin and goal of creation."[40] I would interpret this by saying each divine person has a personality, an infinite field of activity (or form, for example, the form of the Son) that is completely unified with the other fields of activities (the Father and Spirit). God's unbroken wholeness is a dynamic field or matrix of energy with distinct personal fields of activity in which the field of Being itself is the energy of love. Bracken states that "the world of creation originally came into being and still continues to exist within this divine field of activity."[41] While creation exists in God and not apart from God, it exists within the divine field of activity while retaining its own created identity or *haecceitas*, a medieval term used to describe the unique individuation of being.[42]

Matter, now considered as structured fields of activity, and spirit, as energy, help us make sense of death. Energy comprises fields. Once energy dissipates or ceases, the field dissipates or dies—but it does not disappear altogether, that is, it is not annihilated. Rather, what was "matter" (the informational pattern or field) is converted through death to energy and enters the universe as "information" or patterns of information. This information translates into memory in the universe. Memory in the universe then becomes a source of new life and can help generate greater wholeness of life. The "old" fields of energy become "new" fields of activity; the old is incorporated into the new so that new fields of activity (matter) are formed by renewed sources of energy (spirit). Since this renewal of life (evolution) is taking place within the divine matrix (God), the new field formation is always lured into greater unity or wholeness. "Without creatures drawing energy from their environment," writes Denis Edwards, "there could be no emergence of life."[43]

Process theology helps us make sense of the resurrection in a way that classical Aristotelian notions of matter and form could not because of the understanding of being itself. Quantum physics and evolution help us understand the resurrection as reconstituting a new field of activity and new energy. This new theandric—divine-created—energy field *is* the risen Body of Christ.[44] The death of Jesus forms a new matrix of divine-created life within the cosmos. Resurrection into this new form of existence and activity is a new incorporation into the ongoing divine field of trinitarian life, which is a dynamic life of ever newness in love (or infinitely new energy). Can we see the risen Body of Christ as a new pattern or field of activity in the cosmos, a new form of interrelatedness in which many other created fields in the cosmos are joined by a new energy of relatedness? Can we interpret the resurrection narratives of the Gospels in light of this new paradigm? When Jesus appears to the disciples, does the appearance impart a new energy, forming a new pattern of relationship? For example, when Jesus appeared to the disciples on the road to Emmaus, his words set their hearts "on fire," and they were energized into a new union with God and with one another: "were not our hearts burning within us?" (Lk 24:32). Can we see in the resurrection stories a new energy of whole-making and thus new patterns of relationship?

THE RISEN BODY OF CHRIST AND HEAVEN

To bring the revelation of scripture into dialogue with contemporary science is an important challenge today. Otherwise, key doctrines such as the Trinity and the person of Jesus Christ run the risk of becoming incredible in the face of new scientific understanding. Delwin Brown states that traditions are creative insofar as they maintain a dynamic interface between culture and canon. "The viability of a tradition," he writes, "is the vastness of its collected resources, unified enough to sustain needed continuity and diverse enough to create something new for the new times."[45] There is perhaps no more fundamental core belief for Christianity than the risen Christ; the belief that Christ raised from the dead now lives in the cosmos in a new way must empower believers to live in a new way as well.

The event of Jesus' death-resurrection prompted early Christians to identify him as the Christ, God's anointed one. Following Panikkar, I would say that Jesus is the Christ, but Christ is more than Jesus. By this I mean that the life of Jesus is paradigmatic for every human life precisely because Jesus *is* the Christ. I understand the Christ to be the integrated whole or the integrated matrix of divine created energies. This unifying field of energies is at the heart of the cosmos, the innermost center of the cosmos. Rahner grasped something of this idea when he wrote: "When the vessel of his body was shattered in death, Christ was poured out over all the world; he became actually, in his humanity, what he had always been according to his dignity, the heart of the world, the innermost center of creation."[46]

If Christ is the reason for creation, then can we see this innermost "center" as the fully integrated field, the whole theandric-energy complex, out of which created energy fields are generated and to which they are attracted? This is what I believe we are talking about when we speak of love at the heart of the cosmos. We are talking about an energy that unifies, an energizing force that draws together and unites. Love is relational, and the relationship of love is a *pattern* of relatedness, a field of life that is not only generative of life but by its very interpenetration of relatedness generates new life. Love is the potentiality of what can be because relatedness is energy and energy is always renewing itself; hence, love is always new. Christ is the personalizing center of love, the divine field of love that embraces the cosmos. Christ is a matrix of divine created energies that lures created fields into new patterns of unity. Christ is the One integrated field of love into which all other created fields are attracted. Christ is the One who draws the many into One by the power of the Spirit, who *is* the power of love. If Christ is the form of the field, the Spirit is the energy of the field, all flowing from the Fountain Fullness of Love. Hence, the divine trinitarian matrix becomes the center of the cosmos in Jesus the Christ.

But Christ is more than Jesus because Christ is the integrated field of the cosmos into which every created field is attracted. This integrated field is *personal;* it is the integrated whole and hence present to every created field in a unique and indeterminate way. To speak of the personal Christ as the Personal center of the cosmos is to speak of the Spirit as energy, personally present to every living being and creature, the energy that creates fields and fields into creatures and creatures into mirrors of God. Because this energy is full of potentialities, the Spirit of new life is always creating the future. Hence the fullness of Christ is always on the horizon; the complete unification of all that exists into a unified whole is always before us. The whole-maker, the one who lives in Christ, embraces death as "sister," as part of the family of life, because death is the transcendence of limits toward the fullness of life. The most catholic reality, therefore, is death, and the mark of Christian life is to embrace death. Life in the cosmos is drama, and the next act always anticipates something more creative, something new emerging out of the chaos of the old.

Chapter Six

Toward Cosmic Wholeness

The celebration of Easter marks the most incredible event in this history of the cosmos summed up in a brief acclamation: "Christ has died, Christ is risen, Christ will come again." Do we ever stop to reflect on what is being proclaimed: Christ *is* risen, Christ *will* come again. Did not Jesus rise from the dead and return to empower his disciples with a new energy and a new direction? *"Go into all to the world and proclaim the good news to the whole creation"* (Mk 16:15). What is the power of the risen Christ in an evolutionary universe, and how do we understand the return of Christ with a cosmic future of billions or trillions of years? The hope that Christ will come again is often thought of in spatial terms as an entry into the world from outside, as if Christ left the world after his death and will return at some time in the future. But how do we understand Christ's return with the belief that Christ *is* risen—not has risen or will rise, but is risen, now, in the present moment? Is Christ with us "to the end of time" (Mt 28:20)? What does this mean for us, for the earth, the planet, and the cosmos?

The message of Easter is a claim that something new has come into the world from its future. In the time of Jesus many Jews expected a general resurrection at the end of history, an idea supported by Isaiah 26:19 and Daniel 12:2 (cf. Jn 11:24). "But nobody expected the resurrection of a single person in the middle of history," George Murphy writes, "a resurrection that was not merely a temporary revival but a new life (Rom 6:9)."[1] Wolfhart Pannenberg states, "If Jesus has been raised from the dead, then the end of the world has begun."[2] That is, the resurrection of Jesus Christ anticipates the destiny of the cosmos—a new field of energy permeating the cosmos. If the resurrection shows us God's final future, then the one who is raised shows the kind of future God intends. The resurrection happens in the present moment, but it is a present moment bathed in future, a new relationship with God, a new union, a new wholeness—a new catholicity—for the deepening of life.

The key to resurrection is in the title Christ. Christ is the Anointed One, the power of God's love that draws together created being into the divine unbroken wholeness of love. Although we think of Jesus Christ as an individual person, the Christ relates to the Hebrew idea of corporate personality. The Pauline concept of the body of Christ, for example, speaks of a sense of community that goes well beyond the idea of a collection of individuals. Paul writes: "Just as in Adam all die, so also in Christ all will be made alive" (1 Cor 15:22). When Paul speaks of one Adam and one Christ, he is not referring to single individuals but to the whole of humankind *(Adamah)* and the new humankind ushered in by Jesus the Christ. The church fathers also spoke of the Christ as a corporate personality. Augustine wrote on the *totus Christus;* Gregory of Nyssa described humankind as the image of Christ; and Maximus the Confessor wrote of the cosmic Christ as the theandric center of the universe. The Christ therefore refers to the whole and not to an individual person. Jesus Christ is *the* human person who symbolizes the capacity for all human persons to be united and transformed in God.

The resurrection of Jesus Christ speaks of a new future for the whole cosmos, "the invasion of the present by the power of what is yet to come."[3] The pattern of Jesus' life—his whole-making—is the Christ at the heart of the universe, the one who is and who is coming to be. Evolution, as Teilhard emphasized, is not blind, random, or meaningless change. Rather, there is a unifying influence in the whole evolutionary process, a centrating factor that continues to hold the entire process together and move it forward toward greater complexity and unity. The ultimate mover of the entire cosmogenesis is something simultaneously *within* the sequence of beings as tendency, desire, and purpose, and *in front of* the advancing wave of development, beckoning it, as its ideal culmination. Teilhard's faith in Christ led him to posit Christ as the future fullness of the whole evolutionary process, the "centrating principle," the *"pleroma"* and "Omega point" where the individual and collective adventure of humanity finds its end and fulfillment.

The universal Christ could not appear at the end of time at the peak of the world, Teilhard posited, if he had not previously entered it during its development, through the medium of birth, in the form of an element.[4] By identifying cosmogenesis with christogenesis, Teilhard showed that the very being of the world is being personalized.[5] New Being is on the horizon of the already existing now; the Christ is present reality and yet before us, realized and unrealized, whole and incomplete. Resurrection is the necessary death awaiting us for new life to emerge in the cosmos. The old is necessary for the new; death is necessary for life.

CHRIST THE NEW BEING

Christianity has focused so intently on sin and salvation that it has lost sight of Christ as the new creation emerging from within. The dominant Hellenic influence on the shape of Christian thought has imparted an unhealthy otherworldly focus, reinforced by dualistic thinking of matter and spirit, soul and body, as if separate parts come together by the power of God for the construction of the human person. A "parts" mentality has led to an understanding of the whole creation as parts distinctly separated from one another: humans are distinct from trees, Catholics from Jews, men from women, cleric from lay, and the list goes on. A Christology of parts mirrors a cosmology of parts—like Newton's world, in which individual parts are extrinsically related but intrinsically autonomous. Instead of becoming whole-makers, following the example of Jesus, we have become parts people, fragmenting the cosmos into little pieces and setting parts over and against one another. Christianity must move beyond fragmentation if it is to remain true to its identity in the person of Jesus Christ. Paul Tillich wrote that "Christianity is the message of a New Creation . . . the New Being, the New Reality, which has appeared with the appearance of Jesus."[6] Christ is the One who brings a new pattern of life to the universe. Saint Paul wrote, "For neither circumcision nor uncircumcision is anything, but a new creation is everything" (Gal 6:15). Commenting on the passage Tillich claims:

> What it says first is that Christianity is more than a religion; it is the message of a New Creation. Christianity as a religion

is not important—it is like circumcision or like uncircumcison: no more, no less! Are we able even to imagine the consequences of the apostolic pronouncement for our situation? Christianity in the present world encounters several forms of circumcision and uncircumcision. Circumcision can stand today for everything called religion, uncircumcision for everything called secular, but making half-religious claims. . . . But I want to tell you that something has happened that matters, something that judges you and me, your religion and my religion. A New Creation has occurred, a New Being has appeared; and we are all asked to participate in it. And so we should say to the pagans and Jews wherever we meet them: Don't compare your religion and our religion, your rites and our rites, your prophets and our prophets, your priests and our priests, the pious amongst you, and the pious amongst us. All this is of no avail! And above all don't think that we want to convert you to English or American Christianity, to the religion of the Western World. We do not want to convert you to us, not even to the best of us. This would be of no avail. We want only to show you something we have seen and to tell you something we have heard: That in the midst of the old creation there is a New Creation, and that this New Creation is manifest in Jesus who is called the Christ.[7]

Christianity is about future, not salvation as an end in itself or heaven or eternal life—but new life. It is about the fulfillment of promise and hope for a new creation. Although the direction of Christianity is forward movement, we have turned Christianity into historical nostalgia for something lost in the past. It has become backward looking, a remembrance of things past, lodged in the seemingly glorious days of Christendom. We have lost sight of Jesus emerging in history as announcing something new, a new way of being for a new world, a new Big Bang, a new relatedness, making wholes for a whole new future.

To enter New Being we must be grasped by it. It is an openness to grace or rather being poised for grace. Reconciliation is the first mark of the New Reality because the evolutionary world longs for wholeness; it is created for union. The cosmos draws its breath from the hope of reconciliation. While the natural world flows more readily into patterns of unity according to its own natural cycles, we humans are disconnected. We are created for union, but we have the capacity to disconnect ourselves from wholeness. We can refuse to become whole, to grow, and to enter into relationship with other humans and nonhuman nature. To become New Being is to be open to new patterns of relationship, to long for wholeness through union with others.

Reconciliation is death to the separate self for the sake of new life. It is forgetting the past and anticipating a new future through shared goodness. Tillich states that "everybody carries a hostility toward the existence into which he has been thrown, toward the hidden powers which determine his life and that of the universe, toward that which makes him guilty and threatens him with destruction because he has become guilty."[8] In an evolutionary universe we are born with a bias toward hostility because we are incomplete. Evolution is the freeing of our hostile self into New Being. Christ *is* the New Being because he mediates the power of an undisrupted union that heals divisions and separations and creates reunion of one's self with one's self and with the family of creation.

Reconciliation empowers unity, and unity is the emergence of New Being. In following the pattern of Jesus' life we participate in the mystery of Christ unfolding at the heart of the cosmos. Each of us has a liberating and healing power if we are open to becoming liberated and healed within ourselves. The healing of self for the healing of creation is the essential meaning of salvation. To be a healer is to be an evolver, a participant in the new future that is breaking into our midst through the power of love. There is no healing or reconciling, however, without suffering and death. Unless we first understand our hurt, we cannot know our healing. As Ken Wilber notes, death to the separate self is the very thing we resist, because it calls for radical trust in the power of the future and the power of the New claiming our lives.[9]

TRANS-HUMANISM AND THE DESIRE FOR CONTROL

Our present age of anxiety does not hold much room for suffering and death. We consider death an end, not a beginning; suffering is an unnecessary evil rather than a means of transformation. We want to control and manipulate being, to create New Being as an extension of our present, incomplete, and often unfulfilled selves.

We want old being without defects or limits. The emerging trend of trans-humanism promises better, enhanced being, overcoming the limits of being a human person, including suffering and death. This influx of technology into daily life has transformed our patterns of play, work, love, birth, sickness, and death. *Cyborg* is a term of and for our times that maps contemporary bodily and social reality as a hybrid of biology and machine. The futurist Ray Kurzweil anticipates an increasingly virtual life in which the bodily presence of human beings will become irrelevant.[10] Robert Jastrow of NASA believes that "human evolution is nearly a finished chapter in the history of life," although the evolution of intelligence will not end because a new species will arise, "a new kind of intelligent life more likely to be made of silicon."[11]

The influx of technology into daily human life carries with it a desire to transcend the limitations of human life, especially suffering and death. Kurzweil claims that machine-dependent humans will eventually create the virtual reality of eternal life, possibly by "neurochips" or simply by becoming totally machine dependent. As we move beyond mortality through computational technology, our identity will be based on our evolving mind file. By replacing living bodies with virtual bodies capable of transferral and duplication, we will become disembodied superminds.[12] Robert Geraci states, "Our new selves will be infinitely replicable, allowing them to escape the finality of death."[13] This futuristic "post-biological" computer-based immortality is one also envisioned by Hans Moravec, who claims that the advent of intelligent machines *(machina sapiens)* will provide humanity with personal immortality by mind transplant. He envisions that the mind will be able to be downloaded into a machine, "a kind of portable computer (perhaps worn like magic glasses)" that can be installed into a new mechanical body upon death.[14] The advent of a post-biological world is the next step of evolution. He writes: "Sooner or later our machines will become knowledgeable enough to handle their own maintenance, reproduction, and self-improvement without help. . . . Our culture will then be able to evolve independently of human biology and its limitations, passing instead directly from generation to generation of ever more capable intelligent machinery."[15]

Daniel Crevier argues that artificial intelligence is consistent with the Christian belief in resurrection and immortality. Since some kind of support is required for the information and organization that constitutes our minds, Crevier indicates, a material, mechanical replacement for the mortal body will suffice. Christ was resurrected in a new body, he states, why not a machine?[16] Antje Jackelén furthers the religious argument by suggesting that AI technology has messianic dimensions. She notes that the development toward Techno sapiens might well be regarded as a step toward the kingdom of God. What else can we say when the lame walk, the blind see, the deaf hear, and the dead are at least virtually alive? The requirements of the gospel and the aims of technical development seem to be in perfect harmony.[17]

The desire for immortality through artificial intelligence relates to the search for cybernetic heaven. Michael Heim, in his *The Metaphysics of Virtual Reality*, states that "on-line we break free from bodily existence. . . . What better way to emulate God's knowledge than to generate a virtual world constituted by bits of information. Over such a cyber world human beings could enjoy a god-like instant access."[18] Similarly, Michael Benedikt believes that the "image of the Heavenly City is . . . a religious vision of cyberspace."[19] In his view, cyberspace is an extension of religious desires to escape earthly existence. Thus, just as human beings must give up their bodies to attain the heavenly city, so too AI proponents view relinquishing the human body for artificial mediums as a positive step in the evolution of Techno sapiens. This new emerging species bears with it the gospel promise of new artificial life. Geraci states: "Only by eliminating the physical and embracing the virtual can we return to the undifferentiated wholeness of the good."[20]

Technology is advancing evolution at an exponential speed today because it claims to fulfill what religion promises—guaranteed goodness. Biomedical technology and artificial intelligence hope to delay the inevitable—death—and to obtain what religion promises, eternal life and happiness. Through mechanical means we will soon be able to overcome the limitations of the body, including suffering and death, and thus attain artificial eschatological paradise. But a perfectly ordered and controlled world free of suffering is a world ripe for evil precisely because everything is controlled. It is a world where nothing new can happen and thus a world without a real future. It is a world without awe and wonder, without surprise, and thus a world that can be blind to God's grace inviting us into new possibilities for new life.

We cannot stifle the progress of technology—nor should we. Technology has engendered a global consciousness that can be the next step in cosmic evolution, if we direct the use of technology appropriately. If we are inattentive to the power of technology, however, it can easily rule our lives and thwart our capacity for evolving toward greater unity. Christianity with its hope for new life is a technology of the spirit, a harnessing of energy for new creation. This new life, however, is not an individual, privatized, or controlled evolution. It does not happen by plugging "New Being" into Google. It is not a product of knowledge or mind detached from body; it is not a faster chip. It is new wholeness, new patterns of relationships to other beings and to the cosmos. The life of Jesus sets the pattern: mercy, forgiveness, reconciliation, prayer, charity, compassion, kindness, generosity, purity of heart, poverty of being, justice, peace, sympathy, tears, joy, sorrow, an engaged life with other human beings, with creatures, with nature and the stars and all the elements, and a heart attuned to grace radiating through creation. It is awakening to our relatedness to the earth, to other creatures, and assuming our responsibility in this earthly relationship: solidarity with the poor, compassion with the suffering, hospitality for the stranger, treating each and every creature with utmost dignity. It also means living sufficiently without consuming excess amounts of vital resources, conscious that we share this planet with divers peoples, creatures, and elements.

There is no future of new life, no New Being, no real hope of a new heaven and a new earth, however, without our participation. Tillich writes:

The word *resurrection* has for many people the connotation of dead bodies leaving their graves or other fanciful images. But resurrection means the victory of the new state of things, the New Being born out of the death of the Old. Resurrection is not an event that might happen in some remote future, but it is the power of the New Being to create life out of death, here and now, today and tomorrow. Where there is New Being, *there* is resurrection, namely, the creation into eternity out of every moment of time. The Old Being has the mark of disintegration and death. The New Being puts a new mark over the old one. Out of disintegration and death something is born of eternal significance. That which is immersed in dissolution emerges in a New Creation. Resurrection happens *now*, or it does not happen at all. It happens in us and around us, in soul and history, in nature and universe.[21]

Every act of death and resurrection is an act of new creation, an evolution toward greater unity, a participation in the genesis of Christ. We who say yes to the dying and rising of Jesus Christ say yes to our lives as the stuff out of which the New Creation can emerge. Christian trans-humanism values the human person as the leading edge of the evolutionary universe. The whole evolutionary universe is a birthing of Christ through the power of the Spirit, who is the power of wholeness for the whole cosmos. The trans-humanist Christ does not supersede the biological evolution; rather, in Christ biological evolution is fulfilled in its potential for God. Since we are the continuation of Christ in evolution, the positive direction of evolution depends on our choices and actions. We are to give ourselves to Christ and to his cause and values, which means not losing the world but finding the world in its truest reality and in its deepest relation to God.[22]

While the incarnation recapitulates evolution, it is not limited to the human person alone but includes the whole cosmos. In the suffering, death, and resurrection of Jesus Christ the entire creation is brought into a new relationship with God. Paul writes: "For we know that all the rest of creation has been groaning with the pains of childbirth up to the present time. However, not only the creation, but we who have the first fruits of the Spirit also groan inwardly as we eagerly await our adoption, the redemption of our bodies" (Rom 8:22–23). Secular trans-humanism, especially artificial intelligence and biomedical technology, thwart a new cosmic future by focusing on the individual self and its perfection. Trans-humanist technology promises a new self that will ultimately be discontinuous with the old self, one that seeks to overcome finiteness and contingency through the repackaging of information. But we cannot transcend ourselves ad infinitum because we are creatures. We must transcend ourselves because to be a creature is to be oriented toward a goal. As John Haught notes: "Jews, Christians and Muslims generally believe that the universe and our lives within it are the temporal and sacramental expression of an eternal meaning or 'purpose,' the bringing about of something good or the actualizing of value. In these traditions, authentic human life begins with a steady trust that something of everlasting significance is working itself out in the universe and that out own lives are connected to this larger drama."[23] The key here is a "larger drama," a drama of participation not self-fulfillment, a transcendence toward something more, not perfection of limited existence. The danger of auto-enhanced technology is that it leaves the self unchanged. Technologies of the self, whether a cyber self or new genetic self, "are self-asserting rather than self-transforming, enhancing the ego rather than surrendering it to a greater reality and purpose."[24] Ronald Cole-Turner writes: "The danger of technology is that it offers the illusion of a managed grace whereby the self can fix itself up without changing and remaining in control—so we think."[25] We believe we have created the means to expand our control of the self when in truth we have increased only the power of the self to control, leaving the self unchanged yet self-changing, uncontrollable yet more controlling. Technology is not out of control because it is a real power but because "we cannot control what is supposed to control it: namely, ourselves. We lack the inner resources to use these powers responsibly and wisely."[26]

Trans-humanists who look to a post-biological being characterized by mind or computational information threaten to sacrifice the organic whole at the expense of perfecting human intelligence, which they maintain is the core of human personhood. To be a human person is to be in continuity with the whole creation, including material creation. We emerge from the creative process and are related to it. To say that the mind alone is the essence of the human person is to reduce the human person to a silicon chip detached from nonhuman creation. The priority of the mind over matter (cyberspace) not only leads to the death of God (intellect as immortality) but to the death of the human person as *human*, that is, one created for drama, beauty, and ultimate goodness.

Christian trans-humanists see technology as a deepening of human personhood marked by personality, relationality, unity, and transcendence. The core value for Christian trans-humanism is love, which gives meaning to the spiritual center of the human person as well as to the cosmos. We are created to participate in the unfolding new creation through the power of love, which includes death. Technology can alienate and cut us off from the sights and sounds of nature, resulting in loneliness and isolation. The human person, cut off from nature, withers and dies alone with the pain of unfulfilled longing for community.

Christian trans-humanism recognizes a new stage of evolutionary development through technology, but one that has cosmic purpose and shared power. It aims toward a new future not by replicating the self or perfecting its defects but by a transformation of self which requires surrender to God. Christian trans-humanism is self-transcendent, from the isolated self toward community, from the autonomous ego to an essential I–Thou relationship. The new future of life in God symbolized by Christ is a unity in love of humankind in relation with the cosmos. Earth is not left behind but transformed in love and this transformation in love, here on earth, is heaven. What God promises is a new heaven and a new earth not a new heaven without earth.

SACRAMENTAL EVOLUTION

If Jesus is an evolutionary step forward in the development of humankind, evolution does not stop with Jesus. It is an ongoing process, symbolized by the Christ event: "Amen, I say to you, the one who believes in me will also do the works I do and, fact, will do greater works than these, because I am going to the Father" (Jn 14:12). We are not only to continue the work of Jesus, but we are to go forward, advance it, bring it to a new level for the fullness of life in God. Christ is always the New Creation, the New Being forming the horizon of a new future, that is, the fullness of possibilities that lie before us. Future is all that can be in relation to God, who is always the more; God is future, the ever newness of divine love. To speak of Christ as Omega, therefore, is not to see Christ as the final end but as the new beginning. Every act of evolution is an act of Christ, and thus a new beginning. If Christ were the end of created life, then Jesus would not have returned and appeared to the disciples. His appearance, however, meant that the disciples were to continue what Jesus had begun; indeed, they were to surpass the work of Jesus (Jn 14:12). Hence, Jesus establishes the pattern of evolutionary life, but this pattern of life is to generate new life; out of the old is born the new. But the new life is to have new form. If new wine is poured into old wineskins, the skins will burst, as Jesus said; old wineskins cannot contain new wine. Rather, new wine must be poured into new wineskins (Mk 2:22; Lk 5:38). Just as Jesus empowered the disciples to go forth and do new things, so too we are empowered by new life in Christ in order to generate new life in turn. Life in an emergent evolutionary universe is always moving forward toward greater union, and we are the unifiers in the flow.

The sacraments of baptism and Eucharist are sacraments of new life. Every time Christians participate in the eucharistic celebration, they are participating in New Being and the possibility of a New Future for the cosmos. Baptism and Eucharist are sacraments of evolution that empower the New Creation by forging new patterns of divine-human relationship in the evolving cosmos. The Eucharist is the sacrament of wholeness that heals us by accepting our incomplete being into the embrace of God's sympathetic love. One of the earliest New Testament texts, the *Didache*, spoke of the Eucharist as the gathering together of the dispersed people of God in the same place to constitute the eschatological messianic community here and now.[27] Eucharist anticipates cosmic Omega. When we proclaim "Christ will come again," we are saying yes to being the body of Christ now in the world. Christ comes again in us when we respond to the gift of God with the gift of our lives. We become the Christ when we offer our lives as bread for a hungry world, living in the freedom of love and generating new energy in the cosmos, gathering together the multiple fields of being into greater wholes. Eucharist completes what baptism initiates, a new spiritual birth and freedom in Christ.

Because of the Word made flesh all creation is being divinized, Teilhard wrote: "Through your own incarnation, my God, all matter is henceforth incarnate."[28] The Eucharist recapitulates the transformation of the universe in Christ because, in the death and resurrection of Jesus, all is being transformed and drawn into a new relation with God. The Eucharist marks the *beginning* of a new future, not the end. Those who participate in the Eucharist are asked to remember the death and resurrection of Jesus, not as a past event but as the power of the future. The remembrance is an empowerment to go and do the same: to die and rise in this new pattern of life at the heart of the universe that is the Christ. We have domesticated the Eucharist by depleting it of its power to create anew. The dangerous memory of Jesus has become a comfortable memory of piety, not an invitation to costly discipleship for a new future. It does not "challenge self-serving and ideological justifications of the misery of the poor and the victims of war, oppression and natural disasters."[29] Nor does it draw us into solidarity with the poor; victims of violence and oppression; and oppressed creatures of the earth, the peoples, animals, and plants whose well-being is destroyed or threatened. The Eucharist, the sacrament of whole-making, has become the sacrament of division: men separated from women, clerics from the laity, Catholics from non-Catholics. The very sacrament that should challenge us to patterns of relationship has become the primary source of division.

How shall we evolve toward the fullness of Christ? We need to reclaim a eucharistic life for a eucharistic planet. What takes place in the Eucharist must sacramentalize our hope for the universe, union and transformation and a new future in God. A eucharistic community should be a new energy field, a new pattern of relatedness; the joy of being a eucharistic people is the renewal of energy for the sake of transforming relationships in the cosmos. To be a Christian is to be in relationships that promote the flourishing of life. We might think of these new relationships as new morphogenetic fields. Jesus establishes new energy fields of compassion, inclusivity, healing, forgiveness, peacemaking, mercy, and justice. As the Christ, human energy is now integrated with divine energy throughout the cosmos. Baptized into cosmic evolution, the Christian is to be a field integrator, a participant in new possibilities that carry with them creativity and imagination. The practice of gospel values should establish morphogenetic fields of gospel values and, hence, fields of energy that can influence new collective wholes.

The yes of the Christian to the body of Christ is a yes to life in the cosmos, to the earth, the planet and stars, to the diversity of creation and all peoples, to the many religions that seek the ultimate ground of being. The Christian says yes to all of these because all are brought together in the unity of Christ. This is the wholeness we desire, the unity of peace and justice, the dignity of all peoples, respect for all living creatures and life systems. To say yes to this wholeness within us is to participate in Christ the future: "If I do not go away," Jesus said, "the Advocate will not come" (Jn 16:7). We are not to cling to Jesus; we are to let go of his humanity and embrace our own humanity (see Jn 20:17). It is our own humanity that is the dwelling place of the Spirit. The humanity of Jesus is not an idol upon which to project all our expectations, but an icon in which we can see the divine light shining through. Jesus of Nazareth now lives as the Christ, and to the extent that we welcome the Spirit of creativity into our own lives, Christ is born in the universe. Our participation is necessary for the fullness of Christ; without our participation, the Spirit is adrift in the cosmos. Hence, to follow Christ is to enter into a new level of consciousness, of relatedness, and of wholeness. Biological evolution has not ended with us but rather depends on us. We are part of an ongoing cosmic process that demands our commitment.

Chapter Seven

Can the Church Evolve?

Albert Einstein once remarked that science without religion is lame, and religion without science is blind. Although not a believer in a personal God, Einstein could not help but bow before the ineffable mystery at the heart of the universe. His recognition of science and religion as two ways of knowing the one world anticipated the dialogue between science and religion that has developed over the last fifty years. The Catholic Church has been part of this dialogue, engaging top scientists and theologians in conferences on modern science and recognizing that evolution is more than a hypothesis. Despite the many science and religion conferences the church has sponsored, however, it has yet to embrace new scientific ideas as essential to the development of theology. The word *dialogue* means two interacting *logoi*, a crossing over from one world into another for the sake of sharing experience, mutual understanding, and mutual trust; a meeting of horizons, enabling return to one's own world with a deepened horizon of meaning.[1] Dialogue is a form of wisdom when knowledge gained through conversation leads to conversion, a deepening in love, and thus a new way of being in the world. Dialogue that is not self-expansive is self-limiting, and self-limiting dialogue is basically a monologue; essentially, we wind up talking to ourselves. Is the church truly engaged in the dialogue of science and religion, or is such dialogue buffering a resistance to change? When is scientific data sufficient to warrant changes in our theology, not superficial changes but essential changes in our understanding of God, divine action, Jesus Christ, salvation, and eschatology? When does theology become untruth?

The majority of scientists today in areas of physics, biology, and chemistry agree that evolution is true. It is not a theory in the sense of hypothetical speculation; rather, evolution is the way life unfolds and proceeds. Evolution is a dynamic process toward greater complexity that requires chance, law, and deep time. It tells us that change is integral to life, or rather, that without real change there is no real life. Life unfolds from simple structures to complex systems, and this development is not entirely predictable; chance is integral to change. Yet, the direction of evolution is toward greater complexity and hence greater unity; simple isolated structures give way to more complex unions. Today scientists find that most systems are open systems, and the openness of systems means that new things can happen. What we call material reality is an appearance of underlying interrelated fields of energy. Interrelated energy fields form the structure of things, and things are formed by patterns of interrelatedness. Nothing is static; all is related. Change and movement form complex unions, and the extent of complexity is infinite.

So where is God in the midst of this dynamic, evolutionary universe? Based on scripture and tradition, we would have to answer: right in the midst. Scripture tells us that God is Creator, revealed in Jesus Christ, and the Christian tradition says that the Creator is expressed in creation. Creation is a "book"; it *is* God's self-expression. As God expresses Godself in creation, creation in turn expresses the Creator. Every aspect of creation is an aspect of God's self-expression because every creature has its foundation in the Word and is equally close to God. The world is sacramental because the divine Word of God is expressed in the manifold variety of creation; it is a symbolic world and full of signs of God's presence. The universe not only expresses God, but it is fit for God. It is not only related to God, but it has the capacity to receive God within it. From the Big Bang to the present moment the universe is God-filled, divine-love-engendered matter; the evolution of the universe is the coming to be of Christ. Evolution is not opposed to religion; it does not contradict the God of Jesus Christ. Rather, it opens up a new window to the divine mystery. For centuries we thought the cosmos was static, hierarchical, and anthropocentric. The Ptolemaic universe portrayed a perfectly concentric cosmos, a flat earth, and a transcendent, immutable God governing the heavens as the great I AM. The God of Thomas and Bonaventure was the God of the medieval cosmos, and they developed their theologies as profound reflections on Greek metaphysics and medieval science. Thomas's brilliant insights formed the architectonics of Catholic theology, including the life of the faithful and the life of the church.

But the fact is, we no longer live in the medieval cosmos. If we are to be faithful to the integral relationship between God and creation, then we must admit that if the cosmos is in evolution, then God is in evolution as well, or rather, that evolution is God coming to be. God is not static, immutable being but dynamic, relational love: God is eternal, all-embracing divine fields of love, holons within holons, persons within persons—a perichoresis of love within love that is never static but constantly new. The Fountain Fullness (the Father) dynamically generates love that is personal, generative, and unitive, the Son and Word, who is one in love with the Father, holon within holon, bonded by the energizing love of the Spirit, the horizon of love, the harbinger of God's future. It is within these dynamic divine fields of love that creation emerges—not as a thing or an event, but as God's self-expressed love. God speaks God's own mystery into that which is not God to become the glory of God in what is other than God. Because there is a Word in God, creation can exist as an external word; because there is an Absolute Otherness, there can be a relative otherness.[2] Creation is God's poetic Word expressed in the rich diversity of living creatures. The incarnation is not an isolated event but integral to the possibility of creation itself; one is inconceivable without the other. Because of the integral relationship between creation and incarnation, a world without Christ is an incomplete world; the *whole world* is structured christologically. That is, the universe is oriented toward unity in love, toward wholes within wholes, because God is Creator and eternally becoming unity in love. The new science today directs us away from speaking of God as ontological "being," distinct from the world, and orients us to think of God as God-Creator, whose I AM is integrally related to WE ARE: love within love, wholes within wholes. Our existence is God's existence, and to the extent that we truly live, God lives. Without our participation in birthing the divine mystery, God remains a beggar in the cosmos. The evolution of God on planet earth requires our participation in love. We can no longer assume that the God of the medieval cosmos is "up there," hovering over us as a great divine parent. God is within us and is brought to birth by us.

EVOLUTION AND CHRISTIANITY

Teilhard de Chardin devoted his efforts to showing that Christianity is a religion of evolution, and he urged Christians to love evolution and make it their own. However, for centuries Christians have been taught that humans are "pilgrims and strangers" in an alien world (1 Pt:9–12), passing through turbulent seas on their way to their true homeland in heaven. While dualistic thinking influenced the development of otherworldly consciousness, Christians lived with an ambivalent attitude toward the world. We still find this identity of alienation still preached in fundamentalist circles. One Christian website recently stated: "We are living in this world, but this world is not our home (Phil 3:20). We are here, God willing, long enough to need a house to live in, and a job to feed us. But, we are not permanent residents. We are merely pilgrims passing through earth on our way to Heaven."[3] It is this type of literalism, historian Lynn White lamented, that gave rise to our present ecological crisis. Christianity, he indicated, with its emphasis on human salvation and dominion over nature, "made it possible to exploit nature in a mood of indifference to the feelings of natural objects."[4] Christians, he said, have treated the earth as a stage or background for the human story rather than as part of God's plan for salvation.

Is the world opposed to God or the very place of God's revelation? If one turns to the scriptures, one finds little evidence that the world is opposed to God. In the Gospel of John, for example, the "world" has polyvalent meaning.[5] According to Sandra Schneiders, "world" refers first to *creation* itself, as we read in the opening creation account of Genesis (1:1—2:4a). God spoke all things into existence and declared them "very good"; thus, "the 'world' refers to the whole universe emerging in goodness from God's initiative through the Word."[6] The world is also seen as the *theater of human history* "into which every human being is born, including the Word made flesh."[7] The world is our home, the place where we dwell. Third, the world is the place where the *reign of God* unfolds. Jesus prayed to God not to take his disciples out of the world but precisely to keep them safe from evil in the world (see Jn 17:15). The world to which Jesus sends his disciples includes all creation, especially humanity, as it makes its way through history.

Finally, the world is a *synonym for evil*, "the domain and the work of the Prince of this World (see Jn. 12:31; 14:30; 16:11), whom Jesus calls Satan (see Jn. 13:27), the Devil, the Father of Lies who is a murderer from the beginning (Jn. 8:44). Jesus engages in a struggle with this personal evil agency which will cost him his life and which, he warns, will cost his disciples theirs if they take up his project."[8] This more nuanced understanding of *world* underscores a complex arena in which the reign of God and the kingdom of Satan contend for control, and good and evil intimately coexist in our world. Schneiders interprets this tension as the complexity of forces within which the human struggle in the pursuit of God takes place.[9]

The multi-layered meaning of the world as the place of creative holiness and the place of struggle also includes the world as the place of human development. Thomas Merton interprets the world as an *inner* struggle for holiness. In *New Seeds of Contemplation* Merton says that "the world is the unquiet city of those who live for themselves and therefore are divided against one another in a struggle that cannot end." One cannot flee the physical world, he states, because flight from the world "is nothing else but the flight from self-concern."[10] To renounce the world is not to escape from conflict, anguish, and evil but from disunity and separation. Flight from the world is not something we do because the world from which we flee is as much in the cloister as it is in the marketplace. Rather, flight from the world is an attitude of striving for unity and peace in relation to oneself and others. It is a way of being God-centered wherever one finds oneself. According to Merton, there is no true human growth apart from the world and its interacting energies. That is why he challenged the monastic *fuga mundi* that came to dominate religious life and the popular idea: "in the world but not of the world" (1 Jn 2:15–16; Rom 12:1–2). This phrase meant a distancing from the world as the place of ungodliness and worldly humanism at the expense of any religious or metaphysical consideration. It is not the world, the flesh, and the devil that are obstacles to God. It is our refusal to let God be in the world that undergirds rejection of God and the world. Christ proclaimed to the disciples, "*Go into the world* and proclaim the good news to the whole creation" (Mk 16:15, emphasis added). We are not asked to create an alternate world or to reject this one but to divinize and help transform it from within. Teilhard de Chardin struggled with the Catholic view of worldly ambivalence. N. Max Wildiers states that the core problem of Teilhard's thought is secularization, which has led to recognition of the values inherent in earthly and human activity.[11] Although Teilhard rejected any type of "pantheistic bliss," according to Henri De Lubac, he held that "we must love the world greatly if we are to feel a passionate desire to leave the world behind."[12] In his view the problem was the inability to resolve the conflict between the traditional God of revelation and the "new" God of evolution, or, we might say, the inability to refashion Christology for an evolutionary world. Wildiers states, "The conflict we are suffering today does indeed consist in the conflict between a religion of transcendence and a secularized world, between the 'God of the Above' and the 'God of the Ahead,' between a 'religion of heaven' and a 'religion of the earth.'"[13]

Teilhard's approach to the problem of secularity begins with evolution. It is precisely because our world is in evolution that human activity takes on new meaning and importance; human work is integral to evolution. Teilhard saw human activity as the building up of Christ in the world. The zeal of the Christian for the transformation of society, or the revolution in which the Christian is engaged to change the structures of society, is nothing less than evolution toward the fullness of Christ. The key to secularity, according to Teilhard, is found at the very center of Christian faith, in a Christology relevant to the world in which we live, since the universe is organically linked to Christ. Teilhard's solution to the problem of secularity is to rid ourselves of the old God of the starry heavens and embrace the God of evolution. Only in this way, he states, is God truly revealed in the world, which is a divine milieu. In *Science and Christ* Teilhard wrote: "Christians should have no need to be afraid or shocked by the results of scientific research, whether in physics, biology or history. . . . Science should not disturb our faith by its analyses. Rather it should help us to know God better."[14] To reject evolution, in Teilhard's view, is to reject God. Until we come to know God in evolution, we shall find the world a problem. Teilhard envisioned the evolutionary process as one moving toward evolution of consciousness and ultimately toward evolution of spirit, from the birth of mind to the birth of the whole Christ.[15] He urged Christians to participate in the process of christogenesis, to risk, to get involved, to aim toward union with others, for the entire creation is waiting to give birth to God. He opposed a static Christianity that isolates its followers instead of merging them with the masses, imposes on them a burden of observances and obligations, and causes them to lose interest in the common task. "Far too many Christians are insufficiently conscious of the 'divine' responsibilities of their lives . . . giving only half of themselves, never experiencing the spur or the intoxication of advancing God's kingdom in every domain of mankind."[16] Christianity, in Teilhard's view, is nothing short of a daring adventure. We are not only to recognize evolution but make it continue in ourselves.[17] Before Christians thought they could attain God only by abandoning everything. One now discovers that one cannot be saved except through the universe and as a continuation of the universe. We must make our way to heaven *through* earth. Teilhard's imaginary, we might say, is one of "deep secularity." The world in its physical roots is penetrated with Christ.[18] We are to harness the energies of love for the forward movement of evolution toward the fullness of Christ. This means to live from the center of the heart, where love grows, and to reach out to the world with faith, hope, and trust in God's incarnate presence.

Teilhard offers a new social imaginary, beginning with evolution, whereby secular and earthly activity are integrated into the future of the world lying ahead of us.[19] The religious person must be truly secular, because it is only an embrace of secularity that will disclose God. Teilhard's doctrine offers three new perspectives on the problem of secularism. First, his love of matter and spirit is a dual commitment to God and to the world; second, his inclusion of suffering and evil in the forward movement of evolution offers a realistic approach to suffering as part of unfolding life; and third, the participation of humans is essential to the evolution of Christ in the world and the world in Christ. "If we are to remain faithful to the gospel," he writes, "we have to adjust its spiritual code to the new shape of the universe. . . . It has become the great work in process of completion which we have to save by saving ourselves."[20] The Christian response to secularity, therefore, is not to escape or reject the world, nor is it to live with a double standard of values—spiritual and worldly. Rather, the secular is the realm of incarnation, which means Christians must see the world in its divine depth, and that is shown precisely in the worldliness of human activities and earthly affairs. We still do not have a sufficient grasp of relatedness within the cosmos to realize that we are part of the whole and can only find salvific healing within the whole cosmos. Christians today must be truly *catholic*, that is, they must become whole-makers. To be Christian is to be in evolution, and to be in evolution is to participate in the creation of whole-making, to create toward unity in love.

THE REBIRTH OF CHRISTIAN LIFE

Modern physics has changed our understanding of the world and introduced us to an evolutionary wholeness and a whole new sense of cosmic reality. We belong to an implicate order by which the entire universe is unified. The physicist David Bohm writes, "We have to regard the universe as an undivided and unbroken wholeness."[21] Just as the physical world is composed of integrally related particles, we too are integrally related to one another and to nonhuman creation. We live in a web of relationships, and just as we affect this web by our actions, we too are affected by it. What does this mean for the religious person? For the one who follows Christ? We might get some insight by reading the Gospels with "evolutionary eyes." We continue to read the Gospels with eyes conditioned by medieval theology, and we continue to function religiously as if we live in a medieval cosmos. But how do the Gospels speak to us through the eyes of evolution? For one, they speak to us of new life through healing, mercy, and the forgiveness of sins. Throughout the Gospels, Jesus makes wholes where there were divisions (or creates divisions in order to make wholes, such as leaving father and mother for the sake of the gospel); his healing is whole making; his forgiveness of sins restores spiritual wholeness; his mercy and compassion make hearts whole; and his death on the cross reveals God as love that embraces the whole. The Gospels speak of hope and promise, the horizon of a new future that the Spirit is creating in those who are open to evolution in love. Jesus consistently states that nostalgia or regret will thwart the unfolding reign of God. All those who put their hand to the plow and look back are not fit for the kingdom of God (Lk 9:51–61); the reign of God is before us, not behind us. Elsewhere he says that it is important to follow him, to go forward rather than to dwell in the past: "Follow me, let the dead bury their own dead" (Lk 9:60). When Mary Magdalene recognized the voice of Jesus in the garden of the tomb, she wanted to hold on to him, but he exhorted her: "Do not cling to me, for I have not yet returned to the Father. Go instead to my brothers and tell them, 'I am returning to my Father and your Father, to my God and your God'" (Jn 20:17). To be a disciple of Jesus is not to cling to Jesus but to go forth as part of the cosmic family, to enter into new relationships. The message of Jesus can be summed up in several key ideas: make wholes where there are divisions, forget the past and go forward, allow the Spirit to work in you to create a new future; do these things because God seeks a new presence in the cosmos, a new unity in love, peace, and justice. The whole gospel message is based on the advent of new life. Jesus shows us that new life is possible; indeed, the risen Christ is the hope of the cosmos, the Christ who is coming to be in and through us.

To engage evolutionary life as a Christian it is necessary to ask some fundamental questions: Am I a relational being? Am I open to relationships? Am I making wholes? To be a Christian today requires a consciousness of relatedness and a consciousness of evolution. Christian life is a way of being related in the world and to the world. It is recognizing that relationships form the field of gospel values rather than gospel values forming relationships. There is no peace, mercy, forgiveness, or love without persons who exist in relationships of peace, mercy, forgiveness, and love. The gospel of Jesus Christ is the living word of God that continues to be spoken as the word of evolution and in evolution. We humans become the gospel when we embody and personalize the values Jesus established: the pattern of God's emerging presence in history. The more we become whole within ourselves, the more we generate wholes among ourselves. To become a whole-maker is to become wholly centered in God.

It is important to find new language to describe Christian life in an evolving universe. Words like *entanglement, morphogenetic field, holon,* and *holarchy* can help us define new life in new ways. How do we understand our actions as Christians in terms of entanglement or morphogenetic fields? What does it mean to be part of a holarchy, the principle of whole/parts within whole/parts? Can we understand the church, the body of Christ, as a holarchy? How do our actions affect others near and far, perhaps around the globe? Do we know ourselves to be intrinsically related to one another or do others infringe upon our autonomy? We may see a glimpse of this new emerging Christian life in the gospel movements such as Sant'Egidio and Focolare, which seek to bring Christ to birth through new patterns of relationship. The Sant'Egidio website states:

> Friendship among people of different nations and cultures is the everyday way to express this international fraternity. Living this global dimension of life together means both to be open to the world and to belong to one family, the family of disciples. . . . In a world which, at the end of the second millennium, is raising barriers and emphasizing national and cultural differences so much that they become the cause of old and new conflicts, the communities of Sant'Egidio testify to the existence of a common destiny not only for Christians, but for everybody.

Similarly, Focolare seeks unity in love as the basis of Christian life. Its mission speaks to our interrelatedness, to the idea that repeated patterns of behavior create new forms of life, to the fact that our interrelatedness means we influence one another. Even across vast amounts of time and space we affect one another by our actions. The Focolare mission is one of creating holons of unity in love by living in relationships of love and forgiveness, inviting others into union-in-love and thus creating greater wholes. In its section on dialogue among religions the Focolare website states:

> We have become increasingly convinced during the recent decades of dialogue that what the faithful of other religions expect from Christians is a practical witness to the love found in the Gospel. It is not by chance that the golden rule "Do not do to others what you would not have them do to you" is common to all major religions. In the atmosphere of mutual love which accompanies the practice of the golden rule, dialogue may be established. This demands us to "make ourselves one" with the other, to "live the other." This is not just kindness, openness and esteem, it is a practice that requires

the complete "emptiness" of ourselves to become one with the others, to "enter beneath the skin of the other" and understand more deeply what it means for the other to be a Muslim a Hindu a Buddhist. . . .

If love is truly the heart of Christian life, then authentic Christian life can flourish in an evolutionary universe through new patterns of love. What would Christianity *look like*, what impact would it have on the world, if we stopped talking about Jesus Christ and simply lived the beatitudes, creating morphogenetic fields based on the gospel? Could we be the leading edge of this evolutionary universe, as Teilhard envisioned? If we desire the gospel to energize the forward movement of evolution toward greater unity, how can we engage new patterns of relationship to strengthen new morphogenetic fields? Can we form new communities with people of other religions by praying together or worshiping together in such a way that new fields of unity are established? Can we welcome the divorced and remarried, gays and lesbians, and a married priesthood into community as the unfolding vision of God for the transformation of the earth? Can we renew our relationship to the earth in such a way that we stop abusing its resources and begin to love the tiniest of creatures as kin, speaking as voice of creation's voiceless, treating every aspect of nature with utmost dignity? Can we relinquish our selfish patterns of economic wealth and open up our communities to welcome the poor? Can we begin to look at every aspect of human existence as thoroughly interrelated? What we have to do, Teilhard said, "is not simply to forward a human task but . . . to cultivate the world. The world is still being created and it is Christ who is reaching his fulfillment through it."[22] The Christian of today, Teilhard indicated, must gather from the body all the spiritual power it contains, not only from the personal body but from the whole immense cosmic body—air, water, wind, sun, all the elements, and creatures that are the world "stuff" in evolution. We are to harness the energies of love for the forward movement of evolution toward the fullness of Christ. This means to live from the center of the heart where love grows and to reach out to the world with faith, hope, and trust in God's incarnate presence. Belief in God's incarnate presence is belief in a new future, a new creation.

If Christianity is not only to survive but to flourish, it needs a new imagination for the earth community, a new dream for the cosmos, a new understanding of Christ in evolution as the mystery of the whole, which includes other religions, cultures, the whole earth community, and yes, other planets and forms of life. In short, Christianity needs a new direction, one pointing not upward but forward, not toward "heaven above" but to a new future of healthy relationships in the cosmos, a new heaven on earth, which is what Jesus prayed for.[23] The task of the Christian today is to engage the gospel as transformative—a transformed consciousness for a transformed way of life. Christianity must speak to the world of something new emerging from within, new life and a new future, transcending the present world toward a deepened, more fruitful life. The greatness of the Christian way is not attaining some ideal community but enkindling energy for new life. It is witness to the Spirit of God creating anew in our midst, drawing us more deeply into the ever newness of divine love and to unity in love. We should not dwell on utopian ends, a heaven "above," but on the journey itself. It is not *what* we will achieve but the *way* in which we get there because *there* is here. As we evolve toward a new level of religious consciousness, we must *let go of the past* and engage the future, because the future is upon us. Without engagement toward new reality, Christ cannot come to be.

WHOLE-MAKING AND WHOLE-BREAKING

We may grasp the importance of evolution and its impact for Christian life, but the fact is, there can be no real change in the world without corporate change. We may change and grow individually, but we find, as we do so, that we are at odds with others who do not share the same horizon of meaning or insight. As the mind begins to explore the deep mystery of God, the heart begins to change. Insight leads to vision. We see things differently because we ourselves have changed. We begin to know ourselves as free creatures of God set against the stone walls of the institutionalized status quo. This polarizing tension is where we find ourselves in the church today. An evolution of consciousness is emerging in history and in the lives of many men and women committed to the gospel of Jesus Christ. This new consciousness is expansive, inclusive, attuned to the new science, ecologically oriented, and pluralistic in scope. It seeks a new way of being Christian in the world that includes shared power between women and men, intercommunion between Catholic and Protestant churches, reconciliation with the Jews, dialogue and mutual trust with Muslims, recognition and respect of indigenous people, rapprochement with the Anglican Church, and development of needed reforms in the church initiated by Vatican II. It is a new consciousness of whole-making and therefore resists the attitude of divide and conquer. The new emergent Christian consciousness is a consciousness of interrelatedness and a desire to create new morphogenetic fields, new wholes within wholes, in short, a new catholic presence.

This new emergent catholic consciousness reflects a new consciousness of God in the world, an openness to the Spirit as the breath of new life—the God who is creating anew. It is awareness of God who is dynamically engaged in the work of creation open to the radically new. Consciousness is the motor of evolution. The whole evolutionary process, according to Teilhard, is an evolution of consciousness.[24] As consciousness evolves, so does the universe. When the level of our awareness changes, we start attracting a new reality. Because consciousness brings with it a new horizon of meaning, it creates differences. When Jesus of Nazareth appeared in public announcing a new consciousness of God's presence, he became at odds with his fellow Jews; when he forgave sins in the temple or picked corn on the Sabbath, he challenged the Jewish consciousness of God and the Torah. Because consciousness emerges out of the deepest personal center of being, it cannot be suppressed or annihilated; it must show itself by its very evolutionary nature. The new emerging Christian consciousness or, I might say, the new emerging catholic consciousness, cannot be suppressed. Information technology is enhancing the speed of its evolution, and it is taking root at the most basic level of individual lives. As with evolutionary emergence on the whole, the new emerging catholic consciousness is encountering resistance to change on various levels: the institutional church, academic theology, and ecclesial life. On the institutional level the church clings to the Thomistic synthesis with its inherent Greek metaphysical framework. Hence, it supports a three-tiered universe that is orderly, hierarchical, and anthropocentric with distinct orders of being. Within this system there are ontological distinctions between male and female, cleric and lay, religious and nonreligious, body and soul, heaven and earth, God and human. The ontological distinctions supported by the institutional church are rooted in Aristotle's notion of being and hence of matter and form—even though evolution and quantum physics have been around for almost a century. On the level of academic theology, Radical Orthodoxy mourns the loss of the medieval synthesis and chastises Duns Scotus for the demise of the medieval synthesis and the rise of secular theology.[25] Thomas's theology is supremely glorified, as if Vatican II were merely a historical event, and Pseudo-Dionysius is considered the real genius behind Catholic theology. On the ecclesial level, communities are divided among ultramontanism,[26] the Tridentine mass, Catholic intellectual life, and Vatican II. A desire for a strong Catholic identity is challenged by the pluralism of postmodernity and its inclusive spirit of community. On every level, whether it is resistance to new theology or the refusal of pluralism, the inability to embrace Catholic identity as new patterns of relationship reflects an inability to let go of medieval theology and engage the world as science informs us. Hence, there is resistance to relate to God in a new way, in a new world, to see the God of Jesus Christ as the God who does new things, the God of hope and promise.

As I write this chapter, we are in the midst of one of the greatest scandals in the history of the Catholic Church, the sexual abuse by priests of thousands of innocent children. Words fail to describe this despoiling of innocent victims, and the only way to go forth is to name the reality of what went terribly wrong, to forgive, and to help create a new future of relationships that are transparent and mutually accountable. And, at the same time, women religious in the United States are undergoing an apostolic visitation because they are suspected of being unfaithful to the church, wholly secularized, and thus tarnishing the jewel of religious life. Although changes in religious life emerged out of the documents of Vatican II, and not in spite of them, the decline in vocations, the aging of religious communities, and the individualization of religious life have led to the idea that religious life is in need of major reform and should return to its medieval Neoplatonic system of hierarchy and order. In the midst of these crises, the Catholic Church is losing members as it becomes increasingly irrelevant to a world in need.[27] It is difficult to say for certain, but it seems the church is slowly collapsing from within. It is a progressive diminishment, a gasping for air, but nevertheless the church no longer has the body of a runner, aiming to win the prize up ahead (Phil 3:12). Instead of evolving, it is devolving—its very presence is thinning out to the extent that in some areas of the world, such as parts of western Europe, it is dissolving into history.[28] Parishes are closing, religious communities are merging, and many youth are not interested in what the church has to offer. The *Boston Globe* ran an article in 2005 on the state of the church around the world. Portraying a dismal picture of empty churches throughout Europe, the author describes the "withering" of Catholic Europe. Once packed with people, the churches are now dotted only with the elderly on Sunday mornings. The steady erosion of Catholic churches throughout Europe reflects the massive forces of secularization and consumerism, compounded by the scandals of the clergy sexual abuse crisis. While the number of people who consider themselves Catholic throughout Europe remains high, the actual number of people attending mass is low. According to Charles Sennott, author of the *Globe* article, the percentage of Catholics in Germany, France, Italy, and Ireland "who attend Mass regularly has slipped to as low as 20 percent, and in a few cities, like Paris, has reached as low as the single digits."[29]

The depletion of Catholic life in Ireland, Spain, Portugal, and other bastions of European Catholic life is alarming. Ireland in particular has suffered the blows of the sex abuse scandal and the cultural shifts of secularization, and very few seminarians are being trained for ordination. All of these factors have led to a drop in seminarians over all western Europe, and the European Catholic Church does not have a sufficient number of ordained clergy for a sustainable future. Soon the resources required to maintain the church will outweigh the available resources in staff, finances, and personnel. What is the rate of sustainability in a parish that has one priest for six churches? What is the future in a diocese that has gone bankrupt? These are difficult questions. Perhaps we need to return to creation to learn again the complementarity of male and female, the rich diversity of nature with its various species and colors, the meaning of cooperation, mutuality, and symbiosis that enables all of creation to work together for the good of the whole. The peace of creation that draws young and old, rich and poor to sit quietly amid its glorious wonders is a "new cathedral" for many people. The world of nature expresses divine beauty and wisdom through the rhythm of death and life.

Natural death is an interesting phenomenon because the parts of the body begin to die one by one. As each part shuts down, there is a slow transformation taking place. The breath of life that once animated the body begins to dissipate and lifelessness begins to settle in. It is a matter of time before all the organs cease to function and the Spirit of life is released from the body. Death is part of new life. Are we experiencing a necessary death today in the Body of Christ, the Church? Is the Church experiencing a weakness of heart from within because there is no longer sufficient spirit of life to sustain itself? Are we on the brink of resurrection or revolution?

Chapter Eight

The Inner Universe

A crisis is defined as a rapidly deteriorating situation that if left untended will lead to disaster in the near future. We are experiencing crises today on several different levels. On the level of ecology, we are at the brink of an over-stressed planet, excessive energy consumption, and global warming; on the level of economics, the financial crises of the mega-corporations dominate the news; and on the domestic level, there are the crises within families, including infidelity and domestic abuse. On every level of life today there is breakdown and disorder, and it is causing havoc in people's lives. There is no doubt that a crisis can have devastating effects personally and corporately, but it can also initiate new growth and the need for change. A crisis can either terminate a system or signal a new one. In closed systems a crisis functions like a sharp pain; it indicates something wrong in the system or that the system has been disrupted. In open systems a crisis functions like a strange attractor. The idea of the strange attractor arises out of chaos theory, which says that, in open systems, a basin of attraction can spontaneously appear within the system and pull the system into new patterns of behavior over time.

Since evolution operates primarily as an open system, I suggest that the crises we are experiencing, especially in the church, underscore a seismic strange attractor in our midst. Something new is arising within and disrupting the present system, pulling it into new patterns of behavior despite resistance. I identify this strange attractor as a breakthrough in consciousness. We are in the midst of an evolutionary breakthrough toward global consciousness, and it is having profoundly disruptive effects on Christian life, both on the level of practice and doctrine. Like other world religions, Christianity emerged in the first axial period of consciousness, a period marked by autonomy, freedom, and transcendence. Through technology and mass communication, we are entering a new axial period of consciousness that is evolutive, global, ecological, and communal. Rather than responding to these crises by a Darwinian fight or flight syndrome, I think it is better to see the present moment as an invitation to new life. The dynamic newness of God is creating us from the future by way of the heart, that is, God is creating us inside out (cf. Ez 36:26–27). To move through a new consciousness into a new way of life is to discover the inner universe as the source of the emergent Christ in cosmic evolution.

THE DEATH OF JESUS

If we look back over the course of evolution, the fourteen billion year history of the universe, we can see that cosmic evolution is cruciform in nature, as I discussed in Chapter 5. The whole cosmic ascent in consciousness is a transcendent process of death and new life. The death of Jesus recapitulates cosmic evolution. His suffering and death combined into not only a historical event but a cosmic event, because without the death of Jesus evolution would not have meaning, purpose, and direction. Jesus explained, "If I do not go away, the Advocate will not come to you; but if I go, I will send him to you" (Jn 16:7). The departure of Jesus is the gift of the Spirit. The going away of the earthly Jesus is the beginning of the resurrected Christ made possible by the Spirit. One must wonder why Jesus could not stay to finish the work he had begun. Instead, he promises the Spirit to his followers at a moment when his whole mission borders on the brink of disaster. Raimon Panikkar writes:

> The future does not seem bright, his followers will be persecuted. The Master is about to leave without having finished hardly anything while almost abandoning his disciples. The people have abandoned him because it has become too risky to follow him; the synagogue declares him a heretic, indeed blasphemous; the political representatives despise him; and his "own" do not understand him. He has not left them anything durable, no institution; he has neither baptized nor

ordained, much less had he founded anything. He has left both
the Spirit and himself as a silent presence in the Eucharistic
act. He has sent his disciples as lambs among wolves and refuses to change tactics even at the end: wolves are still roaming
about. He promises his followers only one thing: the Spirit.[1]

There is something worth noting about Jesus' imminent departure at a time when his mission was just getting under way and his
disciples were gaining in number. Jesus does not stay around to
complete his earthly work; rather, he promises the Spirit to his disciples, for it is the disciples who will complete his work. "Whoever
believes in me," he had said, "will perform even greater works, because I am going to the Father" (Jn 14:12). Imagine the utter amazement and confusion of the disciples during the final days of Jesus'
earthly life. How were they to perform greater works than Jesus?
Indeed, they feared the loss of their Master and teacher. But Jesus
indicates that evolution is possible because of the Spirit. Through
the power of the Spirit, Jesus' disciples can do greater works than
him, for the Spirit does new things, and only in the Spirit can we
move forward toward wholeness of life in God. Thus, Jesus says to
his disciples, "It is good that I am leaving you" (Jn 16:22). Otherwise, Panikkar writes, "we would make him king—that is, an idol—
or we would rigidify him into concepts, into intellectual contain-
ers. We would turn his teaching into a system, imprison him within
our own categories and suffocate the Spirit."[2] Jesus knew that it
was good that he leave, that he had not come to remain but to
remain in us in the most perfect form, not as a more or less welcome guest foreign to us but in our very being. This is the meaning
of the Eucharist. This is the work of the Spirit and the meaning of
Christ: "I am with you always, until the end of time" (Mt 28:20).
Jesus leaves so that the dynamism of life will not be reduced to an
arid dualism. His departure does not signify the departure of God
from the world but the release of God into the world. The Spirit is
sent into the world to continue the work of Jesus—whole-making—helping to evolve toward unity in love. The Spirit of evolution is released in the cross of Jesus Christ for the purpose of new
life, the transformation of earth into heaven.

The passion narratives indicate that love and freedom go together; to be perfect in love is to be totally free, an uncoerced freedom by which one acts from a spontaneous center of love within.

The Gospel of John particularly highlights this relationship in the passion of Jesus. What leads Jesus to the cross is fidelity to the Father: "I made your name known to them . . . so that the love with which you have loved me may be in them, and I in them" (Jn 17:26). The Spirit who leads Jesus to the cross is the same Spirit who led Jesus into the desert—the Spirit of love, the Spirit who searches the depths of God, who listens attentively to One who is the Fountain Fullness of love. The cross is not about sin, guilt, and judgment but about God. What breaks open in the death of Jesus is the revelation of God's humility, the God who embraces this evolutionary universe in love and desires the cosmos as beloved. Otherwise we would have to ask: Why did the Father not save the Son from a violent death if God is perfect love?

We cannot grasp the meaning of Jesus' death without considering the role of God in his death. Hans Urs von Balthasar has described the cross as the nature of divine trinitarian love. The self-gift of the Father to the Son reflects a self-emptying already within the heart of God in such a way that we may think of the cross first in the heart of God before it is in the heart of creation. The very act of creation reflects something of a "divine crucifixion," for in creation God reveals the divine power to be God's own unconditional love for the world. The act of descending into what is nothing—creation—in order to express Godself is God's humility, God's condescension, God's going outside the divine riches to become poor. The cross is key not only to sin and human nature, but to God. The cross reveals to us the heart of God because it reveals the vulnerability of God's love. Balthasar writes: "It is God's going forth into the danger and the nothingness of the creation that reveals his heart to be at its origin vulnerable; in the humility of this vulnerability lies God's condescension (condescensio) and thus his fundamental readiness to go to the very end of love on the cross."[3] The passion is the revelation of the heart of God in the heart of Jesus disclosing the mystery of the cross as the overflowing fountain of God's love. As Bonaventure noted, the mystery of the cruciform love of the Son leads us into the very heart of the mystery of God. This idea is captured by Jürgen Moltmann's insight on the cross as *the* core of theology: "When the crucified Jesus is called the 'image of the invisible God' the meaning is that this is God and God is like this. God is not greater than he is in this humiliation. God is not more glorious than he is in this self-surrender. God is not more powerful than he is in this helplessness. God is not more divine than he is in this humanity. Everything that can be said of God is to be found in this Christ event."[4]

God is not a lonely deity at the top of a medieval cosmos, spinning the stars and governing the heavens; rather, God is selfless love poured out by the power of the Spirit as dynamic newness of love desiring a beloved—to make whole, to unify, to evolve toward an infinite depth of love. God acts in creation as God is in Godself—dynamic love. It is out of this love that we are and continue to be created. Walter Kasper describes the cross as the revelation of the divinity of God, the very power of God to heal, make whole, to emerge in evolutionary creation. "God need not strip himself of his omnipotence in order to reveal his love," Kasper writes. "It requires omnipotence to be able to surrender oneself and give oneself away; and it requires omnipotence to be able to take oneself back in the giving and to preserve the independence and freedom of the recipient. Only an almighty love can give itself wholly to the other and be a helpless love."[5] Thus God's love, shown to us in the weakness and powerlessness of the cross, is the power of love to heal and transform death into life. God is most godlike in the suffering of the cross. God does not remove suffering but transforms it from within to what is godly—to a new future. Dietrich Bonhoeffer, writing from prison, understood that the powerlessness of God on the cross is the power of God in creation: "God lets himself be pushed out of the world onto a cross. . . . He is weak and powerless in the world and that is precisely the way, the only way, in which God is with us. . . . Only the suffering God can help."[6] It is precisely God's self-emptying that empowers creatures to do new things, to evolve.

To understand the cross as the very locus of theology, the revelation of God, puts a few things in perspective. For one, it tells us about the God who is coming to be in this evolutionary universe—not a God of self-righteous judgment or a superior king but a humble God whose selfless love is born out of inner freedom. Second, the cross recapitulates Jesus' life of whole-making. It symbolizes the dynamic of evolution: isolated existence must yield to greater union. Third, the cross indicates that new life cannot emerge without suffering and death. God suffers the new creation not out of need but out of an abundance of love, out of sympathy for the beloved. The only way to evolve toward greater wholeness is to let go and die to those things that hinder the emergence of love from within. Such death involves suffering, accepting pain as part of the birthing process to richer life. Pain rends, but it is in separating that love gathers the scattered pieces and creates anew. The very thing we fear—death—is the beginning of what we desire—wholeness. Sin is the refusal to love and hence the refusal to die; it is the protest against relatedness and community. Those who cannot love cannot suffer, for they are without grief, without feeling, and indifferent. We suffer when we experience in suffering the lack of love, the pain of abandonment, and the powerlessness of unbelief. The suffering of pain and abandonment is overcome by the suffering of love, which is not afraid of what is sick and ugly but accepts it and takes it into itself to heal it. "Anyone who enters into love, and through love experiences the inextricable suffering and the fatality of death, enters into the history of the human God."[7]

The profound reality here is that the problem of suffering is not God's problem; it is ours. When we try to control suffering or eradicate it; when we aim for the perfect human life free of defects and disease; when we seek immortality through artificial means trying to bypass death, we stop being human and nature also stops being itself. Jesus' death on the cross is the most authentic statement of created life—it speaks to us of the wild love of God, the drama of evolution, and the trust that is needed if a new future is to be realized. The illogical cross is the logic of God. It is the logic of self-involvement that requires a self-emptying, a space within oneself for new life to be born. By domesticating the cross, we strip the Godliness of God, the wildness of divine love that refuses to be controlled or manipulated. God's love is the untameable terror of the Holy New. To be a whole-maker, to evolve, is to embrace this Spirit of love, to trust that love is greater than death. Bonaventure wrote: "Christ on the cross bows his head waiting for you, that he may kiss you; his arms outstretched, that he may embrace you; his hands are open, that he may enrich you; his side is open for you that he may let you enter there."[8] If we desire to move from conflict to resolution, from divisions to unity, then we must ask: Can we be wounded for the sake of love? Salvific love that heals and makes whole is born out of human infirmity. Salvation takes place in what is weak and fragile. Unless and until we grasp the inner core of evolution as a necessary death we will continue to spiral in violence and fragmentation. Belief in God incarnate is belief in the wildness of divine love to seize us from within, turn us upside down, and move us in a new direction.

POVERTY OF BEING

The journey into the inner universe is a journey into love, but even more, it is a journey into the poverty of being. The first beatitude that Jesus proclaimed was "blessed are the poor in spirit, theirs is the kingdom of heaven" (Mt 5:3). What is poverty of spirit, and how does poverty bestow the gift of heaven? The type of poverty that Jesus announced was a poverty of dependency. We come from God and we belong to God; hence, the whole of our lives is dependent on God. To be dependent on God is to be dependent on the things of this earth, on other people; it is to be in relationship. Poverty is not so much about want or need; it is about relationship. Poverty impels us to reflect on our lives from the position of weakness, dependency, and vulnerability. It impels us to empty our pockets—not of money—but the pockets of our hearts, minds, wills— those places where we store up things for ourselves and isolate ourselves from real relationship with others. Poverty calls us to be vulnerable, open, and receptive to others, to allow others into our lives, and to be free enough to enter into the lives of others.

To be a truly human person is to be poor because to be human is to be created. Life is radically contingent; nothing has to be the way it is. Everything is gift. Poverty is not a definition of the human condition but a description. Michael and Ken Himes write: "The discovery of one's finiteness is the recognition of one's poverty. When one grasps the 'iffiness' of one's existence, the shocking fact that the source and foundation of one's being is not in oneself, then one knows oneself as truly poor."[9] Many people know they are finite. Few, however, will admit they are poor. To say that I am poor is to confess that I am dependent on others for the source of my existence and for every breath of air I breathe. My poverty says to me that I do not have to exist at all. I am here in this place at this time, but it could have been otherwise. I may never have existed, or I may have existed in another place at another time. The very fact that I am here is more than mere chance or coincidence. I am here not because I choose to be here, as if I could have chosen otherwise. I am here because God's love has brought me into being—and I am here. If I could know this love, then I could embrace this moment as the moment of my poverty. I could realize in my poverty that I am free to birth to God—I can glorify God. Thomas Merton wrote:

> For it is God's love that warms me in the sun and God's love that sends the cold rain. It is God's love that feeds me in the bread I eat and God that feeds me also by hunger and fasting. It is the love of God that sends the winter days when I am cold and sick, and the hot summer when I labor and my clothes are full of sweat. . . . It is God's love that speaks to me in the birds and streams; but also behind the clamor of the city God speaks to me in his judgments, and all these things are seeds sent to me from his will. If these seeds would take root in my liberty, and if his will would grow from my freedom, I would become the love that he is, and my harvest would be his glory and my own joy.[10]

Each creature is a gift of God with an intrinsic value that is unique to itself. Poverty of being binds us to God, opening us up to the heart of God, who is the origin of every good gift. To be poor is to be filled with an inner freedom to receive graciously the very gift of life itself. Poverty expands being because it makes us receptive to the gift of life; the more open we are to receiving, the more we are able to be with and for others. The poor person is one who loves because in the poverty of being one sees the truth of being held in love. Poverty, therefore, means radical dependency; we come from another and are dependent on another for the very existence of life.

All of creation is contingent or essentially related, not just the human person. "The human person has no more claim to intrinsic being than a plant or animal, a star or a stone," the Himes brothers write.[11] Humans do not have a solo part in the creation story; all creation is grace-filled reality. It is a sacrament of God's abundant love freely shared. The doctrine of creation out of nothing *(creatio ex nihilo)* is not a claim about how the universe came into being but why it came into being at all.[12] It discloses the fundamental poverty of the universe. The universe has no intrinsic ground for existence.[13] It is a free gift of God's overflowing love. Poverty allows us to contemplate the goodness of God in creation because it makes us free to see things for what they are, gifts of God loved-into-being. Only one who can taste the world and see it as an expression of God's love, can renounce the spirit of possessing it. On the level of human relationships poverty allows us to be open to one another, to receive and share with one another. Poverty is the basis of personhood because it involves kenosis or self-emptying. Only care for one another truly humanizes life. Barbara Fiand claims that "the blessedness of the poor [the economically poor], that which has them stand in solidarity, is their need and their knowledge of their need. It is this need that renders them open, receptive, grateful."[14]

Francis of Assisi saw himself as part of creation. Poverty enabled him to realize his solidarity with creation. Instead of using creatures to ascend to God, he found God in all creatures and identified with them as brothers and sisters because he saw that they had the same primordial goodness as himself. Francis considered himself a brother to all creation. All creation was his family. This was not some type of romantic love, but a real insight into his relatedness to the stars, moon, sun, wind, and earth. Everything spoke to him of God, and he found God in and through created things. Leonardo Boff explains that such poverty "lets things be what they are; one refuses to dominate them, subjugate them, and make them the objects of the will to power."[15] For such an embrace of poverty one must renounce the instinct to power, to have dominion over things. It is the desire to possess that stands between true relatedness between persons with each other and with all creation. Francis lived in creation *sine proprio*, not without things, but without possessing things. Through poverty Francis recognized that, as a creature, he was "not over things, but together with them, like brothers and sisters of the same family."[16] The poor human person dwells in poor creation, reflecting God's gracious and generous love. The Himes brothers claim:

> Utterly dependent, creation is divinely gifted. Thus, to see creation as a whole or any creature in particular as what it is, namely, totally dependent on the gracious will of God, is to see revealed the grace which is its foundation in being. Since everything that is exists because of the free act of God—the overflowing *agape* that is the source of all being—then everything is a sacrament of the goodness and creative power of God.[17]

The poverty of created existence reveals the richness of divine presence, and the poverty of the human person is the fullest revelation of God. How we live as poor persons in evolution is how creation can evolve toward the fullness of love.

THE JOURNEY INTO GOD

Evolution toward wholeness—the Christ—is first an evolution toward inner wholeness and wisdom, knowing oneself as a creature of God. In *Soul's Journey into God* Bonaventure describes the path to true Christian knowledge not as one of intellectual knowledge but wisdom. To make this journey one must be a poor person in need of God. In the prologue Bonaventure writes:

> I invite the reader
> to the groans of prayer
> through Christ crucified . . .
> so that he not believe
> that reading is sufficient without unction,
> speculation without devotion,
> investigation without wonder,
> observation without joy,
> work without piety,
> knowledge without love,
> understanding without humility,
> endeavor without divine grace.[18]

Bonaventure begins with prayer as the key to relationship with God. Prayer is the expression of intimacy with God; it shapes who I am and what I become. Prayer unfolds the inner universe in which I am created and which I create. It is the most direct line of communication to my interior reality in which every denial of that reality is a diminishment of myself. Prayer, therefore, requires an honest encounter with God. When I fail in this honesty, I diminish myself because I fail to allow the fullness of God's Spirit to move within me and thus I fail to come to my authentic self in God.

In *New Seeds of Contemplation* Thomas Merton wrote that we are divided between a true self and a false self. The true self is the self God created and the one known most intimately by God.

However, we often prefer the false self, the self that is hidden from God and who God knows nothing about, a self that is cut off from life-giving relationships with others.[19] The false self dominates our attention when we lack self-knowledge. It is the selfish self that seeks its own security and protection, the self I think I need to be that is far from God and unknown to God because God did not create it. Prayer is the discovery of the true self, the self created by God who in its "self-ness" utters a unique word of God. Out of this self the universe is born, and out of this universe life can grow in abundance. The person who comes to know himself or herself as a creature of God discovers the true self, and in this self is the freedom to become an authentic person uniquely loved by God.

If prayer is the beginning of self-knowledge, conversion is the dynamic state of turning toward wholeness. Conversion (*metanoia*) refers to the way one arrives at a new way of looking at a situation or a new understanding of an issue. Conversion is not something we "do" as an action. Conversion is a way of becoming more authentically human—through an interior attitude of "turning" from a selfish self toward a God-centered self, from self-preoccupation toward the other as the basis of self. Because we are integrally related to one another and to nonhuman creation, conversion is the maturity of accepting interdependence as the definition of human life and of life in the universe. Conversion is supported by poverty of being and humility. Poverty is recognizing our need for God, and even more so, knowledge of our need, which renders us open, receptive, and grateful. It is an attitude of acknowledging that all is gift given to us by God. It is the sister of humility by which we accept ourselves and others as creatures, as finite beings. Poverty is a virtue that belongs to all who are authentic persons, those who live in relationship and who can receive and respond to another. Those who are full of themselves, whether materially, emotionally, or psychologically, are "sent away empty."[20] The goodness of God's creation cannot be theirs, for they experience no need and therefore cannot receive.

True poverty creates community because it converts self-sufficiency into creative interdependency where the mystery of life unfolds for us. Only those who can see and feel for another can love another without trying to possess that other. Poverty is that free and open space within the human heart that enables us to *listen* to the other, to *respect* the other, and to *trust* the other without feeling that something vital will be taken from us. Conversion to poverty and humility is the foundation of wholeness because it is the movement to authentic love—a movement from isolation toward union, from individualism toward community, where Christ is birthed in the web of life.

CONTEMPLATION

Bonaventure's journey, which begins with prayer and self-knowledge, is a journey into the soul, where the divine image and the power to love lie in unique splendor. As we let go of the need to control our lives and enter into relationship with God, we discover the truth of our being, and in this truth is our freedom to be. Hence, our interior liberation becomes a freedom to contemplate God. This freedom opens up the spiritual vision of the heart, and we begin to see the life of the universe and our own lives with new eyes. To contemplate God is to contemplate the beauty of the universe, the unique details of every living being; it is to love. Nothing in creation is accidental or excessive; nothing is worthless or trivial. "The world is charged with the grandeur of God," wrote Gerard Manley Hopkins.[21] Each and every thing, no matter how small or seemingly insignificant, is of infinite value because it images God in its own unique being. Hopkins spent long periods of time in nature gazing at the wonder of each created being. His poem "As Kingfishers Catch Fire" eloquently describes this in-dwelling love being in love:

> As kingfishers catch fire, dragonflies draw flame;
> As tumbled over rim in roundy wells
> Stones ring; like each tucked string tells, each
>   hung bell's
> Bow swung finds tongue to fling out broad its
>   name;
> Each mortal thing does one thing and the same:
> Deals out that being indoors each one dwells;
> Selves—goes itself; *myself* it speaks and spells,
> Crying *What I do is me: for that I came.*

> I say more: the just man justices;
> Keeps grace: that keeps all his goings graces;
> Acts in God's eye what in God's eye he is—
> Christ—for Christ plays in ten thousand places,
> Lovely in limbs, and lovely in eyes not his
> To the Father through the features of men's
> faces.[22]

The poet's gaze is not a roughhewn sketch of nature but a deep contemplative gaze that gets to the truth of reality. Contemplation is indwelling love, a centering of one's heart on the heart of the beloved. To see with contemplative eyes is to see the truth of each being—loved uniquely and distinctly into being by God. We cannot purchase such a gaze; it cannot be programmed in a robot or attained online. Such a gaze requires encounter with another, meeting the other in love and having space within one's heart to receive this love as the very source of life. The gaze that gets to the truth of reality takes time. A technological mindset cannot comprehend that "dead time," of which modern technology tries to rid us, is often the arena of grace. Kathleen Norris observed that "it always seems that just when daily life seems most unbearable . . . that what is inmost breaks forth, and I realize that what had seemed 'dead time' was actually a period of gestation."[23] In our feverish obsession to fill our lives with more devices that give us what we want, instantly, without effort or engagement, do we cut ourselves off from the graced dimension of ordinary life?[24] When we fail to love, we fail to suffer the pains of new birth and thus we fail to live justly with compassion for the poor, small creatures and the world around us. As Leonardo Boff reminds us, the cry of the earth is the cry of the poor.[25] When we set ourselves over and against others, seeking to control or dominate others for selfish reasons, we destroy the web of life by the will to power. We reject our place in the web of life including the cosmic earth and all creatures, because we reject the call to love.

INNER WISDOM

The soul is the immense power of the universe. Within the vast space of the soul all time, all desires, all imaginations, and all creativities are held together in a single "still point" where the divine and human meet. Love is the gravity of the soul, the force of attraction by which the soul evolves into the greater wholes of beauty, harmony, and order. If there is movement toward wholeness in the universe, then it is first a movement toward wholeness of soul. Wholeness is the integrated field of energy whereby all bodies are joined together by a luminous thread of love. This can take place only when each soul discovers its own power to expand and hence its power to unite. Cosmic unity is first self-unity; this is the core of the Christian spiritual journey. To participate in the flourishing of life in the universe is to discover first the inner universe; indeed, the secret of the universe lies within. The poet Rainer Maria Rilke spoke of the inner universe from which all life flows, the universe that thrives on solitude and presence, attentive to the wonders of life. Within "The Buddha in Glory" he writes:

> Now you feel how nothing clings to you;
> your vast shell reaches into endless space,
> and there the rich thick nectars rise and
>   flow.
> Illuminated in your infinite peace,
>
> a billion stars go spinning through the
>   night,
> blazing high above your head.
> But in you is the presence that
> will be, when all the stars are dead.[26]

What is this presence within each one of us that more than sustains us and bestows personality, uniqueness, and immortality? Is this not the Christ waiting to be born? Bonaventure spoke of mystical death as the goal of the spiritual journey. Encountering the crucified God is not an escape from corporeality, he indicated, but the acceptance of mortality as a symbol and concretization of absolute generosity and self-communication. To journey into God is to become one in love with God, to become crucified in love, like Christ, whose selfless gift of love shows us the capacity of the human person to love for the sake of new life. The more we come to know God, Bonaventure said, the more we are drawn beyond ourselves, leaving behind the intellect and understanding and relying only on desire. The mind gives way to the heart and we are drawn to the One whom we can never fully understand but whom we love. For Bonaventure, "mystical death" is brought about by the grace of the Holy Spirit: "Whoever loves this death can see God. Let us, then, die and enter into the darkness. . . . With Christ Crucified let us pass out of this world to the Father."[27]

Mystical death is death to the superficial world, that is, the world that appears to the naked physical eye. It is rebirth in God, being drawn into the mystery of God through the power of the Spirit, who opens the eyes of the heart to see the truth of things. At the highest stage of union one passes over into the silent hidden depths of divine love, into wisdom. All flesh is silent, darkness prevails, and the fire within the soul blazes with new light. Wisdom is knowledge deepened by love. It is knowledge of the heart by which the heart sees rightly what is invisible to the eye:

> But if you wish to know how these things come about, ask grace not instruction, desire not understanding, the groaning of prayer not diligent reading, the Spouse not the teaching, God not man, darkness not clarity, not light but the fire that totally inflames and carries us into God by ecstatic unctions and burning affections. This fire is God, and his furnace is in Jerusalem; and Christ enkindles it in the heat of his burning passion.[28]

The journey into the inner universe of the soul is a journey into wisdom. It is the inner eye of love that sees the depth of divine goodness hidden in ordinary reality. We cannot find wisdom in a book or on a website. Wisdom cannot be taught, because it is a gift of the Spirit; it is the highest gift of knowledge whereby one knows by way of love. The wise person travels the earth as if in a dark room; one walks slowly, carefully, touching each object to experience it and know it. The wise person takes nothing for granted and lives in creation with wonder, awe, humility, thankfulness, and receptivity to goodness as the essence of being itself. The wise person lives from an inner depth of love. Such a person does not simply accept life as a given but anticipates each moment as a new creation.

Wisdom constantly searches the depths of everything, even the depths of God. That is why wisdom can only be found when all else has disappeared, when we relinquish the need to grasp and control, to manipulate and succeed, to possess material things for security. When all fears die and the soul is stripped to its essential being alive, then wisdom unfolds as the beacon of light from within that begins to see this world with new vision and a new heart. Instead of standing in the world looking for God, one stands in God and looks out at the world. God is no longer the other; rather, the world becomes other and appears as an imperfect reflection of the Truth that has become the soul's dwelling place.[29]

To attain wisdom is to transcend all intellectual understanding. Knowledge may bring us to the door of God, but it is wisdom that leads into the heart of God. "Christ goes away," Bonaventure wrote, "when the mind attempts to behold this wisdom through intellectual eyes; since it is not the intellect that can go in there, but the heart."[30] The problem is that we do not educate for wisdom, for knowledge that leads to greater wholeness and thus for the flourishing of life. We do not educate to form "whole makers," as John Haughey explains. Rather, we overload the human brain with millions of bits of information that need to be processed and stored. The brain is bombarded each day with all sorts of information through books, Internet, e-mail, television, radio, ipod, podcast. Information is rapidly generated in bite-size bits that the human brain must quickly process with no real time to think or connect, no real time to discover the greatness of the soul, the power of wholeness within oneself. The disconnected inner life unravels the whole universe.

The cross is where the wisdom of God is revealed, shattering all other forms of knowledge and opening one up to the depth of mystery. This wisdom of God "is mysterious and hidden." It is given only to those who are prepared to receive the Spirit of new life within them. The one who travels the path of the cross is a *perscrutator* ("one who searches through"); like a seeker of fine pearls, the wise person searches for truth with the inner eye of love.[31] To attain such wisdom is to attain a height of union in love, to enter into silence and death. As Bonaventure stated:

> Now such love divides, puts to sleep, and lifts up. It divides, since it cuts away from any other love because of the single love for the Spouse; it puts to sleep and appeases all the powers and imposes silence; it lifts up, since it leads to God. And

so man is dead, where it is said: *Love is strong as death* (Cor 8:6), because it cuts away from all things. Man, then, must die of this love in order to be lifted up.[32]

The cross is the paradox of the universe, and the human paradox as well. What seems scandalous and illogical is the revelation of divine light. What appears fragile and broken in the shattering of Christ's body is the release of divine wisdom. The light of God's wisdom is revealed in darkness, silence, suffering, and death. Only one who has learned the path of love through poverty and humility can see this wisdom hidden in the cross. One must be on the spiritual journey to God to know the depths of God's love hidden in the depths of creation. The wisdom of the cross shatters all other forms of knowledge and opens one up to the depth of mystery. True knowledge of created reality, therefore, is rooted not in the intellect but in love; it is personal and relational. To know beyond knowing or to attain that knowledge beyond knowledge is to pray. Love goes further than knowledge, and the type of love that is the highest knowledge is wisdom that imposes silence on the intellect and appeases all its powers.[33] One must become as dead in order to see into the heart of things; wisdom is knowledge not of the intellect alone but the feeling of what is known. Only one who can let go of possessing knowledge can really know this world as the heart of divine love unfolding in evolution. True knowledge is bound up with death, and unless one is willing to "die to the ego" in order to attain union with the other, truth remains elusive. Truth is not a given but must be arrived at; it is not a thing but a disclosure. True knowledge is attained through union in love, and without love there is no truth and no real grasp of true reality.[34] In wisdom one sees truth, and in seeing truth one is set free. Wholeness in love is the heart of wisdom, and one who strives to become whole in love will see the world in its unfolding beauty.

The more we enter into the silence and darkness of the divine mystery within our souls, the more deeply we enter into the heart of the world. Without the inner journey we struggle between relationship and autonomy, connectivity and individualism; without the inner journey we are pulled apart by the forces of the world. This pulling apart outwardly can only lead to disrupted lives, fragmented by ungodly forces of selfishness and power. The only way to evolve toward greater wholeness is to let go and die to those things that hinder the emergence of Christ from within. The very thing we fear—death—is the beginning of what we desire—wholeness. Suffering and death call us to return to ourselves from the land of idolatry, which we create as "the world," and to live inwardly as human persons with our immense power to expand into wholeness. Unless we come to know ourselves and our capacity to love, we dwell in mediocrity, apathy, distrust, isolation, and disconnectedness. Out of this mediocrity is the desire for self-preservation and security. Without the necessary inner death there is no inner transformation and hence transformation of this universe we call home. Francis of Assisi saw death as the necessary element for true life: "Blessed are those who die the first death," he wrote, "for the second death will do them no harm."[35] Life is a series of deaths; every choice is a thousand renunciations.[36] The journey to the inner universe, the soul's immense power, requires a thousand deaths along the way. Death is liberation into wholeness and into life. Without the deaths in our lives, there is no wisdom or truth, just the blind force of darkness.

A NEW BIRTH OF CHRIST WITHIN

The journey to wisdom is a process of rebirth. It is a death to the selfish self and a new centering of the heart in God. Out of this new center of love, which is wisdom, comes a new birth, a new relatedness, a new way of being in the world. The soul reborn into wisdom is the soul able to love another, to be for another; it is the soul that no longer fears death because it has embraced death as part of life. Such a soul is truly free to live for others. God evolves in the universe and brings it to its completion through the cooperative co-creative "great work" of human beings. Living from a deeper center within, Christians go about urging all reality toward the Omega, to the final synthesis that is constantly growing within them. What we seek is not the appearance of God in the world but the shining of God through creation, a "diaphany" of God radiating through a world that becomes transparent. The diaphanous appearance of Christ in and through every creature of the universe is encountered in a loving act of surrender in which Christ becomes the "Thou" complementing our "I." Now awakened to a new consciousness of Christ's universal presence, each Christian discovers his or her own self-realization and full maturity in "being-with-Christ." Christ becomes the unifying and integrating center in creation as each person seeks his or her self in Christ and thus in one another.[37] Therefore, "it *does* matter what man does, for only through his action can he encounter God."[38] Human action is to help evolution advance in every field of enterprise—business, science, education, law, agriculture, social sciences, cultural, and artistic pursuits—all of which are involved in a transforming process much greater than ourselves. We are not called to relate to a God without a world. To love God we must also love what God loves. We are called to love this created world as God loves it. We are to help transform this universe in Christ by seeing Christ in the universe and loving Christ in the heart of the universe.

Although the inner universe is the discovery of each human soul as the expanding power of the universe, it is also the discovery of divine wisdom birthing the church. The new evolutionary breakthrough in consciousness is at odds with the medieval world in which the church thrives. But the Middle Ages are long over. Thomas Aquinas is dead; Bonaventure is dead; and the medieval cosmos no longer exists. The new breakthrough in consciousness cannot sustain the myth of God "above" or the story of the fall as the reason for Christ. It cannot support a theoretical or speculative theology that is abstract from the concrete world of evolution; it cannot flourish in a sterile environment of laws and books, nor can it thrive with an all-male monarchy for government. The new consciousness of love at the heart of evolution calls us to let go, embrace our poverty as human beings, and trust the Creator Spirit in our lives. Just as each soul must journey to God through the cross, so too the church must undergo a necessary death, a soul-searching journey, into wisdom. It must empty itself within in order to receive the Spirit of new life, the life of the risen Christ.

Without the necessary death that empowers transcendence toward unity in God, the church remains divided within. "If a house is divided against itself, that house cannot stand" (Mk 3:25); however, the love of God endures forever. That is why the inner center of evolution, the Christ who is coming to be, is finding a home outside the institutional church—in those who are living the Christ and giving witness to this mystery not by word but by example. If we are not prepared to participate in the evolving reign of God, then it will given to others who are prepared to receive the mystery within them, who can awaken to the Spirit of newness in love and travel the path of wisdom. Eye has not seen, nor ear heard what God has prepared for those who love without counting the cost (cf. 1 Cor 2:9), for those who seek justice and peace, who desire an earth transformed in love; a new heaven and earth will be theirs.

Chapter Nine

Christ the Living One

The new universe story, with its expansive reach back fourteen billion years and its openness to billions of years of new life, is truly awesome. "When I look at the heavens, the moon and the stars you arranged," the psalmist writes, "who am I that you should care for me, You who put all things under my feet?" (Ps 8) Just as the psalmist marvels at the expanse of the heavens, we too must ask, how wide is our vision of God? How deep is the divine mystery for us? When I look at the divisions in the church and religious life today, both ideologically and theologically, it seems that the divine mystery is not very deep at all. All of us want to own a piece of the mystery, claim it as our own, defend it like property, and fight for it at all costs. But God is an incomprehensible mystery of love, a love so infinitely deep that words fail, a depth of love that eludes all human grasp, a love infinitely breathless. God is Most High and most intimately related to us. The more we are in union with God, the less we know God by way of the intellect, for only the heart can enter the unfathomable mystery of the God who is love.

When we ask about following Jesus Christ today, we must ask this question in view of the breathless, dynamic, infinitely energizing love of God, who is the inner source of evolution. Because Christ is first in God's intention to love, creation is always the beloved of God. Christ is not accidental to creation or an intrusion to an otherwise perfect universe but its inner ground and goal. Christ is not ordered to us, Bonaventure said, we are ordered to Christ.[1] Christ is the reason *for* the world. All of creation has its source and goal in the fruitful creative love of God. From the Big Bang onward (or even before the Big Bang, if there is a "before") the whole cosmos is incarnational. Christ invests himself organically with all creation, immersing himself in the heart of matter and thus unifying the world.[2] The world is not blindly hurling itself into an aimless expansion; rather, this evolutionary universe is meaningful and purposeful because it is grounded in Christ, the Word of God.

If this world is God-centered love, then how come we resist our participation in its evolution? If cosmic implicate order is one with divine implicate order, then why do we reject our interrelatedness with God and with one another? The reality of interrelatedness held out to us by science today demands a new consciousness of participation. Life in the universe is social by definition. We do not exist as isolated monads; we are interrelated centers of matter and energy. The consciousness of interrelatedness is part of the new emerging second axial period. Ecology, economy, and community mark this new axial consciousness, a desire to belong to the whole. In this new axial period, being is defined not by what something is in itself but by what it is in relation to another. It is a new emerging I-Thou relatedness. Whereas first axial-period consciousness functioned within the heuristic of a closed system, second-axial-period consciousness functions within the heuristic of an open system.

While God is the open system of all open systems, the dynamic Trinity of love open to creation, institutionalized Christian life has functioned as a closed system. A closed system is limited in growth because it is closed to environmental input required for effective operation; it relies only on the resources within the system. However, an open system takes inputs from the environment, transforms them, and releases them as outputs in tandem with reciprocal effects on the organization itself. Open systems are contingent on their environments, which in turn influence the systems' organization. That is, the organization becomes part and parcel of the environment in which it is situated. To say that the institutional church is a closed system is to say that changes in culture—inclusivity of women on all levels of life, respecting the choices of gays and lesbians, recognizing divorce and remarriage as potentially healthy choices, among other developments—have not made a difference in the systematic life of the church. Many people have become disillusioned by the intransigence of the church and have opted out. The end result is that many people are spiritual but not religious. Spirituality is important to their lives, but they do not want to be affiliated with an institutional system unable to develop in both doctrine and practice. In a reflective article on physics and faith, Barbara Taylor Brown compares the institutional church to Newton's world, a vast machine made of parts and obeying fundamental laws, a world easily controlled and manipulated. She writes:

> Human beings were so charmed by the illusion of control Newton's metaphor offered that we began to see ourselves as machines too. Believing that Newton told us the truth about how the world works, we modeled our institutions on atomistic principles. You are you and I am I. If each of us will do our parts, then the big machine should keep on humming. If a part breaks down, it can always be removed, cleaned, fixed and replaced. There is no mystery to a machine, after all. According to Newton's instruction manual, it is perfectly predictable. If something stops working, any reasonably competent mechanic should be able to locate the defective part and set things right again. . . . Our "God view" came to resemble our world view. In this century, even much of our practical theology has also become mechanical and atomistic. Walk into many churches and you will hear God described as a being who behaves almost as predictably as Newton's universe. Say you believe in God and you will be saved. Sin against God and you will be condemned. Say you are sorry and you will be forgiven. Obey the law and you will be blessed.[3]

When we look at the life of Jesus Christ as a system, we have to say that Jesus' life was an open system—new relatedness, new hope, new life. As he encountered the poor, the sick, sinners, the wealthy, he discerned their faith and saw the reign of God taking root outside the chosen Israel. His fidelity in love, which led him to the scandalous cross, sent a shock wave through his disciples—God cannot be controlled or predicted. God does new things and one must attentive to the Spirit of love to engage in the newness of life. Jesus' mission was forward looking, toward a new way of being in the world, a new humanity for a new creation. New life demands new spirit, as Jesus proclaimed: "Salt is good, but if salt has lost its taste, how can its saltiness be restored? It is fit neither for the soil nor for the manure pile; they throw it away" (Lk 14:34–35). His message of God's reign signaled a new openness to God's indwelling love. The closed system of the Pharisees and Sadducees was "old wine" that was not to be mixed with the wine of new life. "No one puts new wine into old wineskins; otherwise the new wine will burst the skins and will be spilled, and the skins will be destroyed" (Lk 5:37).

In light of Jesus' openness to a new way of being God-centered in the world, it is baffling that the church developed as a closed system. Rules, fixed order, established hierarchy, and juridical legislation have rendered the church almost impervious to evolution. It is simply closed to new influences from the outside. All systems have boundaries, a fact that is immediately apparent in mechanical systems such as a watch, but the boundaries of open systems are more flexible than those of closed systems. Open systems interact with their environments; closed systems are rigid and largely impenetrable. A closed system views organizations as relatively independent of environmental influences; problems are resolved internally with little consideration of the external environment. Thus the closed system of the institutional church struggles to protect the mystery of God's ineffable love from the winds of evolution, even though God's incarnate love is source and goal of this evolutionary cosmos.

A closed institutional system trying to control an open evolutionary spirit can only lead to disorder within the system. The openness of any system is its own survival and growth. The more an open system is stifled, the more it will seek new influences in the environment because the nature of open systems is precisely in their openness to new sources of life. Christ is the openness of all life to life, and the overflowing love of the Spirit abounding throughout creation draws others into this life. When the human person, whose openness to life flows out of being image of God, is dominated by power or control, such a person will seek new life elsewhere.

Charles Taylor in his magnum opus, *A Secular Age*, challenges the myth of secularism as the death of religion. The idea that modernity, science, and democracy have advanced in some form of human flourishing at the expense of God and spirituality, he writes, is unconvincing. Taylor follows the trajectories of modernity from the Enlightenment to Romanticism to scientific materialism and finally to the counter-Enlightenment unbelief of Nietzsche, who rejected the benevolence and egalitarianism of modern humanism as offshoots of Jewish-Christian morality. "The positing of a viable humanist alternative," Taylor writes, "set in train a dynamic something like a nova effect, spawning an ever-widening variety of moral-spiritual options, across the span of the thinkable and perhaps even beyond."[4] Taylor argues that Western modernity, including its secularity, is the fruit of new inventions, newly constructed self-understandings, and related practices; it cannot be explained in terms of perennial features of human life. He traces the winding path of secularity through the social imaginary, the picture of the world that holds us captive, expressed by the way people imagine their social surroundings in images, stories, and legends.[5] In his view secularization did not kill off religion, since the depths of humanism have survived as spiritual values amid pluralism and differentiation. Consequently, religion no longer functions as a hegemonic power, at least in the West. Although religion is concentrated in personal belief and practice, Taylor shows that God is still very much present in the world, if only we look at the right places and allow the mind to open itself to moral inquiry and aesthetic sensibility. Instead of disappearing, he writes, God is now sanctifying us everywhere, including in ordinary life, our work, in marriage, and in the daily spheres of life. God is very much alive.

CHRIST THE STRANGE ATTRACTOR

It is the aliveness of God in the appearance of the secular that undergirds the rise of postmodern spirituality, and to some extent, New Age spirituality. The return of God into secular space is manifested in the personal spiritual quest and the longing for I-Thou relatedness that is sought through different religions and the many names of God. The desire for community, relationality, common good, care for the earth, and the fullness of life marks the postmodern seeker. Technology has afforded a new collective consciousness whereby cultures and religions are entering into new creative encounters. There is a new plurality in our midst and a new unity, a convergence of centers of consciousness in the evolutionary process. Cultures and religions are coming together in order to seek a common ground for future development. This new global consciousness challenges the religions to bring about a new integration of the spiritual and the material, of sacred energy and secular energy into a total global human energy.[6] Thus it encourages dialogue, community, and relationship, with a growing awareness that each person is something of the whole. No longer is the human person content with the subjective, reflective critical awareness of first axial period consciousness. Now, one is in need of relatedness.

Technology has empowered religion to become an open system, and because religion has now become a new channel of life outside the institution, Christ too is emerging in new ways. For example, in *Eat, Pray, Love* Elizabeth Gilbert embarks on a search for wholeness after a failed marriage. Hitting rock bottom she begins to pray, and as she prays she begins to discern an inner voice, God's voice, reassuring her that whatever happens "there's nothing you can ever do to lose my love."[7] After eating her way through the culinary delights of Italy, she goes to India to live in an ashram. There she learns how to quiet her inner conflicted soul through meditation. As she practices meditation, she begins to experience God in a deep and personal way. "The only thing between me and God was . . . nothing." Her deep, personal, and mystical experience of God in India reflects the postmodern sentiment of bricolage. "I think you have every right to cherry-pick when it comes to moving your spirit and finding peace in God," she writes.[8]

Although Gilbert never highlights Jesus Christ, her entire journey is "catholic"; it is one of whole-making. As she herself becomes whole, healed of a broken heart, she radiates wholeness to those around her. Toward the end of her journey she recounts an earlier dream assuring her of God's intimate presence:

> I saw that my heart was not even nearly full, not even after having taken in and tended to all those calamitous urchins of sorrow and anger and shame; my heart could easily have received and forgiven even more. Its love was infinite. I knew then that this is how God loves us all and receives us all, and that there is no such thing in this universe as hell, except maybe in our own terrified minds. Because if even one broken and limited human being could experience even one such episode of absolute forgiveness and acceptance of her own self, then imagine—just imagine!—what God, in all his eternal compassion, can forgive and accept.[9]

Gilbert stands for a whole generation today who seek spirituality apart from institutionalized religion. She is not an exception to the norm; rather, she is reflective of it. By the end of her journey she is renewed in love, and through renewal of love, she engages the world around her in positive, life-giving ways. For all practical purposes, she participates in christogenesis. Through her, an inner freedom of love emerges and flows into new positive relationships. She helps build up community and makes friends with those whom she encounters along the way. Her spiritual quest reflects twenty-first-century spirituality with its trans-institutional commitment to the divine mystery at the heart of all life and the search for inner healing, wholeness, and community.

Recently I have become familiar with a global initiative called 10.10.10, which seeks to unite all people in a common mind and heart for the welfare of the planet and of human life on earth. The announcement of this event on the powerofone.org website states: "Become the change, transform the world." The organizers hope that 10.10.10 will mark a new collective energy, a desire to move beyond divisions and conflict toward a world of unity and peace, a new *E Pluribus Unum* connecting people and peoples from everywhere (virtually and physically) as *the Power of One*. This global, interreligious event reflects the new religious complexified consciousness that is emerging in the second axial period. Instead of belonging to a single tribe or religion, people now see themselves bound to one another and the earth in oneness of heart. Religions of the first axial period serve the human capacity for transcendence by helping us go beyond the isolated self to the relational self: the I–Thou relationship.

The new spirituality emerging today is a deepening of consciousness for a new integral way of being in the world. From my perspective I describe this new religious consciousness as a new "catholic" consciousness, a consciousness of whole-making that invites greater unity, forgiveness, reconciliation, peace, charity, kindness, mercy, and compassion. It is a new *zeitgeist* of Christ in evolution, a new breath of the Spirit. The reign of God is coming into the world not only through the front doors of a church but increasingly through human hearts outside the doors of a church. How do we know it is *Christ* in evolution? Jesus proclaimed, "You will know them by their fruits" (Mt 7:16, 20). Those who live in Christ bear the fruits of love, peace, charity, kindness, forgiveness, compassion, and reconciliation; through their lives God is born into the world in new ways, through new relationships, through greater unity. This new birth of God from within is a deepening of consciousness, a new relatedness furthering evolution toward unity in love, toward Christ.

One way to understand this new emergence of Christ in evolution, outside institutional religion, is through chaos theory.[10] As I discussed in Chapter 1, chaos theory describes dynamical systems highly sensitive to initial conditions. In open systems (or systems far from equilibrium) spontaneous basins of attraction can appear that pull the system into new behaviors or new patterns over time. Small changes in initial conditions can have profound changes over time. Although chaos signifies disorder, such disorder is really new order emerging in a way that is not predictable or deterministic. This new order may not be visible at first, but over time it appears as a fractal or pattern that repeats itself, producing a new form, similar to a morphogenetic field.

If we understand Christ in evolution as openness to new life, then events like 10.10.10 are strange attractors in our midst, new "Christ fields" that are appearing spontaneously, pulling local currents of human energy into new patterns of community, oneness of heart, and relationship with the earth. These emerging Christ fields are new basins of attraction, transcending institutional religion, signaling a new religious consciousness, a new God-centeredness that inspires and empowers co-creativity for a new humanity and a new earth. The emerging Christ fields are holons, whole parts, a consciousness of participating in the whole earth, the whole cosmos. They are indicating to us that we live in a web of relationships, and just as we affect this web by our actions, we too are affected by it.

Today the new strange attractors—the Christ fields—in our midst are developing patterns of sharing, community, cooperation, mutuality, healing, justice, and peace. They are quietly hidden throughout the world; they do not make the headlines because they are simply fostering goodness in the world, helping the world to evolve toward greater unity in love. Those who seek to be part of these new basins of attraction are open to new ways of being in the world; they are not threatened by new relationships, nor do they fear loss of their individuality. Rather, their oneness of being opens them up to dialogue and sharing with others different from themselves. They desire to be whole-makers, to live cooperatively and compassionately, to share the energies and resources of life. They are willing to evolve toward new organic, cosmic life, not alternative cyber life, as trans-humanists like Ray Kurzweil anticipate, but an ultrahumanism that furthers the truth, beauty, and goodness of earthly human life. While some postmodern seekers are Christian, others are not. What they share in common, however, is the practice of resurrection.

THE ROLE OF CHRISTIANS

While new emerging strange attractors or Christ fields are sprouting up in unconventional ways, I do see a particular role for Christians in this evolutionary process of christogenesis. As Saint Francis of Assisi once remarked, "It is a great shame for us, servants of God, that while the saints actually did such [great] things, we wish to receive the glory and honor by merely recounting their deeds."[11] Similarly, of what use is it to live a closed Christian life while the world evolves into something greater. Baptism immerses us in cosmic evolution in such a way that we have a responsibility to evolve and to participate in the birth of Christ within: "All of you who are baptized into Christ have clothed yourselves with Christ" (Gal 3:26–27). We are baptized into whole-making, into community through trinitizing love, love that is generative, expressive, and unitive. When we say that Christ is first in God's intention to love, we are saying that the whole evolutionary universe from the beginning is Christ. Those who follow Jesus are to be healthy whole-makers and to help make creation healthy and whole as well. A healthy life for a healthy cosmos requires receptivity, openness, and compassionate love that reaches across the lines of difference and accepts the other as part of oneself because together we are one in this cosmic body of Christ. Barbara Taylor Brown writes:

> There is another way to conceive of our life in God, but it requires a different world view—not a clockwork universe in which individuals function as discrete springs and gears, but one that looks more like a luminous web, in which the whole is far more than the parts. In this universe, there is no such thing as an individual apart from his or her relationships. Every interaction—between people and people, between people and things, between things and things—changes the face of history. Life on earth cannot be reduced to four sure-fire rules.

It is an ever-unfolding mystery that defies precise prediction. Meanwhile, in this universe, there is no such thing as "parts." The whole is the fundamental unity of reality.[12]

Christian life cannot sustain itself in a cosmic, evolutionary universe as a tribal, isolated phenomenon, a closed system. Rather, it must open itself up to realize that every person and created being is fundamental to relationship with God. Our encounter with Christ is always grounded in our life together. Christ emerges as the concrete, historical, personalizing center of this evolutionary universe when each person gives birth to Christ within and allows Christ to shine through humble, fragile creation. If we understand the Christ to be source and goal of the universe, then we can say that the whole of natural evolution is coming under the influence of Christ, the physical and personalizing center of the universe, through the free cooperation of human beings.[13] The desire for wholeness lies deep within the human heart and the heart of the cosmos. However, we must surrender to the wildness of love and free ourselves from the grip of death that controls our deepest fears. The birth of Christ can only take place through liberation of the human spirit.

The way toward greater cosmic wholeness is evolution toward inner wholeness. This wholeness is the still point of wisdom deep within which is the birth of Christ. To live in the mystery of Christ is not necessarily to speak about Christ but to live in the grace of surrender, the poverty of being, and openness of heart—to live in the vulnerability of love. As I indicated in Chapter 4, our relation to God is a new life in "existence for others" in such a way that we not only continue the work of Jesus but through the life of the Spirit we evolve toward greater unity. If we can allow the Spirit to take hold of us and liberate us from our fears, anxieties, and desire for power and control, then we can truly seek the living among the dead; we can live in the risen Christ who empowers us to participate in this new creation. We must wake up from closed, self-protected, mediocre lives and trust in the humble love of God.

The way of the Christian is the way of the crucified Christ. Harvey Egan writes: "Christians must take seriously that resurrection has not been predicated of any historical figure with any degree of credibility other than Jesus of Nazareth. Exclusive and singulat indeed is this salvific activity of God in whom one finds the Father's 'yes' to the human situation."[14] To live in the spirit of cruciform love in the midst of pluralism is to promote mutually affirming relationships among different peoples, religions, and cultures. The particularity of Christ that separates Christians from non-Christians must be the center of union. Simone Weil describes the existence of separateness in a world that is characterized by the existence of intermediaries that lead from one to the other and hence to God. Using the example of two prisoners separated by an adjoining wall, Weil wrote: "The wall is the thing which separates them, but it is also their means of communication."[15] If Christ separates Christians from non-Christians, then Christ is also the basis of unity where the christic life becomes the "adjoining wall" of love uniting what is separated. Christ is love incarnate, the divine embrace of differences in mutual relationship that does not reduce one to the other. Rather, where there is love there is distinction of persons, and this is the basis of union. Christian life is to be lived in the midst of plurality from a new depth of unifying love. It is the Creator Spirit, who weaves together the cosmic body of Christ, the "holon-maker" who searches the depths of God in a variety of languages, cultures, and religions. Where there is the Spirit there is the divine Word expressed in the rich variety of creation, and where there is the Spirit and Word there is the Fountain Fullness of love. Christ symbolizes this unity of love; hence, the fullness of Christ is the creative diversity of all that exists held together by the Spirit of luminous love.

A CONSCIOUSNESS OF EVOLUTION

Being Christian today in a world of differences not only calls for a new consciousness of relatedness but a new *consciousness of being in evolution*. Evolution must be at the heart of a new Christian story, because God is in evolution and we are in evolution as well. We are not yet complete, and Christ is not yet complete. Teilhard envisioned the evolutionary process as one moving toward evolution of consciousness and ultimately toward evolution of spirit, from the birth of mind to the birth of the whole Christ.[16] He urged Christians to participate in the process of christogenesis, to risk, to get involved, to aim toward union with others, for the entire creation is waiting to give birth to God. He opposed a static Christianity that isolates its followers instead of merging them with the mass. Christianity was not meant to be a closed, tribal religion but a cosmic liberator, a generator of greater wholes. Teilhard wrote, "Do we realize that if we are to influence it [the world] . . . it is essential that we share . . . in its drive, in its anxieties and its hopes?"[17] Teilhard said that the role of Christians is to "divinize" the world by our actions, immersing ourselves in the world, plunging our hands into the soil of the earth, and touching the roots of life. His deep secular humanism is a "mysticism of action" that is the core of Christian life.[18] Before, he said, we Christians thought that we could attain God only by abandoning everything. We now discover that we cannot be saved except through the universe and as a continuation of the universe. We must make our way to heaven *through* earth.[19]

By bringing together evolution and incarnation in a single vision, Teilhard reshaped the meaning of gospel life. The gospel call to "leave all and follow me" no longer means leaving the world but "returning to the world with new vision and a deeper conviction to take hold of Christ in the heart of matter" and further Christ in evolution. "The world is still being created and it is Christ who is reaching his fulfillment through it."[20] We are to help generate Christ fields as personalizing centers of unitive love.

LIBERATED IN LOVE

The Christian challenge today is to engage the gospel as transformative, to be whole-makers in a world divided on every level. Beatrice Bruteau describes a shift in consciousness from a domination paradigm to what she calls a Holy Thursday paradigm marked by mutuality, service, and Christian love.[21] To be "in Christ," she writes in *The Grand Option*

> is to enter into Holy Thursday by experiencing some death and resurrection, letting an old modality of consciousness die and seeing a new one rise to life. It is to abandon thinking of oneself only terms of categories and abstractions and seeing oneself as a transcendent center of energy that lives in God and in one's neighbors—because this is where Christ lives, in God and in us.[22]

CHRISTIANITY IS A RELIGION OF THE FUTURE

In Jesus, God's self-communication to creation explodes into history. Evolution assumes an explicit direction. God evolves the universe and brings it to its completion through the instrumentality of human beings. Jesus is the Christ, the climax of that long development whereby the world becomes aware of itself and comes into the direct presence of God.[23] What we see in Jesus is that the future of the material universe is linked to the fulfillment of the community of human beings in whom the world has come to consciousness.[24] We are "cooperative co-creators," and our participation lies at the basis of a healing world, a world aimed toward the fullness of God.

We are not called to relate to God without a world. To love God we must also love what God loves. We are called to love this created world as God loves it. We are to help transform this universe from within by seeing Christ in the heart of matter—in all peoples, creatures, elements, stars, and galaxies. Such vision requires openness to new relationships, new ideas, abandoning messianic expectations, accepting incompleteness as part of life, recovering the capacity of wonder, and living in the primacy of love. Unless we realize the Christ in our own personal lives, however, we shall continue to suffer the violence of blind evolution. We have the capacity to heal this earth and bind its wounds in love, but do we have the desire? Evolution is speeding up in the universe, and we are moving into a new level of religious consciousness that is more global and pluralistic in nature. Does Christianity have something distinct to offer, or are we too worn out by internal divisions and a complex theological tradition? Do we long at times for the old fixed universe? We are called to be whole-makers, to evolve by uniting, growing, and becoming more complex. We are not to seek the living among the dead. Rather, we are to forge a new future, a new hope, a new life that begins with our own lives. We are Christ in evolution, the Living One who continues to appear in new ways, the frontier of the future. We are asked to contemplate Christ, to penetrate the truth of Christ in the community of humankind and in the cosmos, to live in openness to the Christ mystery, God's unfathomable love incarnate. In *The Grand Option*, Beatrice Bruteau brilliantly describes the emergent Christ:

To enter by our transcendent freedom into Christ and to become a New Creation means to enter by faith into the future of every person and into the very heart of creativity itself, into the future of God.

To be "in Christ" is to abandon thinking of oneself only in terms of categories and abstractions by which one may be externally related to others and to coincide with oneself as a transcendent center of energy that lives *in* God and *in* one's fellows—because that is where the Christ lives, in God and in one another.

To be "in Christ" is to experience oneself as an initiative of free energy radiating out to give life abundantly to all, for that is the function of the Christ.

To be "in Christ" is to be an indispensable member of a living body, which is the Body of Christ.

To be "in Christ" is to be identified with the Living One who is not to be sought among the dead, for the Living One is the One who is Coming to Be.

If I am asked then, "Who do you say I am?" my answer is: "You are the new and ever renewing act of creation. You are all of us, as we are united in You. You are all of us as we live in one another. You are all of us in the whole cosmos as we join in Your exuberant act of creation. You are the Living One who improvises at the frontier of the future; and it has not yet appeared what You shall be."[25]

Conclusion

Recently, I participated in a seminar with a group of highly successful business men and women who manage large financial firms and investment companies. The purpose of the seminar was to explore the intersection of faith and business practices. How does one's faith influence decision-making in the business world? The seminar participants were interested in the role of ethics, but most of them kept their faith separate from business life. They attended the seminar to discuss how to integrate faith into daily life and the importance of spiritual values in business practices. While traveling to the seminar, I started reading Thomas Friedman's book *Hot, Flat, and Crowded*, gaining insight into the economic and ecological meltdown brought about by rampant consumerism and the desire to emulate American lifestyles in developing countries throughout the globe. According to Friedman, and many others since the energy crisis of the 1970s, we have entered a new era in which the depletion of energy supplies due to excess demand will have serious consequences for the future around the globe. It is not the world we once knew, according to Friedman, and the future is going to be rather bleak if we continue our present trends of energy consumption.

I conclude *The Emergent Christ* on the note of business and energy because our world runs on business and the choices we make affect our future. For too long we have compartmentalized God, keeping God safely ensconced in a heavenly realm. For many people, faith has been a private matter, not a public statement or personal witness of belief. One wonders, however, if religion is the root cause of our present energy crisis. The classical notion of God's providence over the world has, over the centuries, slipped into an "otherworldly" God who is not at home in the cosmos. Is an otherworldly religious consciousness responsible for the present "hot, flat, and crowded" earth? It seems to me that religious otherworldliness has generated an in-between space for a functional atheism. There is a distinction between God and world, a space between God and world; one can go to church and pray on Sunday, but the nine-to-five routine during the rest of the week is centered on personal needs and desires, as if God did not exist. *The Emergent Christ* was written to offer a new view of God in relation to a world of change. God is not the unmoved mover, but the source and goal of evolution.

It is interesting that Friedman describes a new era of energy, albeit not a positive one, since available energy is being used up at an unsustainable rate. But there may be a new way to consider energy, not only sources of energy for consumption, but spiritual energy that shapes our choices for consumption. God is the energy of new life, and we need to rediscover God as the source of new life. Evolution has changed our understanding about everything we once knew, not only ourselves and our world, but God as well. For theology to resound the harmony of the spheres, it is helpful to play religious music in the key of "D" (for Darwin). Evolution is not contrary to religion; rather, it frees religion from its Greek metaphysical constraints. Life is narrative to the core, and the story of God and creation continues to unfold through us. What I have tried to show is that a dynamically changing world flows out of a dynamically changing God. As Karl Rahner noted long ago, creation and incarnation are not two disparate and juxtaposed acts of God or two separate events of God; rather, creation and incarnation are two moments and two phases of the *one* process of God's self-giving and self-expression; the God who creates is the God who saves.[1] In this respect, the whole creation beginning with the Big Bang is incarnation. Evolution is the process of unfolding life, from matter to spirit; it is the genesis of Christ, as Teilhard de Chardin described. I have tried to show that the God of evolution is in evolution. Change is integral to God because God is love and love is dynamic relatedness. God is eternally becoming ever newness in love, and God's ever newness in love is the inner source of evolution toward newness and greater union in love. Haught writes: "Evolution occurs because God is more interested in *adventure* than in preserving the status quo."[2]

The process of evolution as divine love incarnating matter is expressed as the movement toward greater unity; the many flow into the one. God comes to be at the heart of matter because creation is intended to be the fullness of love. Christ is the centrating factor, as Teilhard explained, the basis of unity that is both immanent and transcendent to material reality. Thus Christ is the unifying principle of the whole evolution. In Jesus of Nazareth the emergent Christ comes to explicit consciousness so that Jesus Christ becomes the exemplary evolutionary person. Jesus recapitulates the whole evolutionary process as one of whole-making. Just as evolution proceeds toward more complex unions or greater wholes, Jesus appears as the whole-maker, the one who reconciles divisions and heals broken lives. Through the life of Jesus we see what it means to be *catholic* in the broad sense of this word. It is to heal and make whole and thus help unify creation in love.

The death and resurrection of Jesus anticipates what is intended for the whole universe: union and transformation in God. The resurrection is about new life and shows that new life is possible if we are willing to die to the old self and engage a new life for a new future. Resurrection is not an otherworldly, future event; rather, it is the this-worldly future breaking into the present moment through a radical choice for life. Death anticipates resurrection because it is the necessary contingent for new life and new relationship with God. The wholeness that we seek in this evolutionary creation, this new catholicity, is possible if we are willing to engage the moment as self-gift. Without the giving of ourselves to something greater than ourselves, nothing new can happen, nor can we evolve toward wholeness by healing the divisions among us and within us. The greatest challenge of our age is not to discover extraterrestrial life but to discover our own inner lives. For various reasons we have lost touch with our inner selves. Some people have been lulled by the routinization of religion; others have simply abandoned religion; and still others are absorbed by the black hole of consumerism. The crises that we are currently facing are, in my view, crises of the human heart. We have become disconnected interiorly— our heads from our hearts, our bodies from our spirits—so we are disconnected exteriorly, not only in our relations to one another but to the earth. A radically disconnected ego can become a selfish one, and until we can find ourselves connected at the root core of our lives, we shall suffer the consequences of selfishness. Of course, one does wonder where the church is in this "hot, flat, and crowded" earth. Stuck in the Middle Ages and unable to evolve, the church symbolizes a culture of self-serving interests and unbridled power, and yet it symbolizes what this evolutionary creation hopes for, union in love with the God of love. I have pondered and still wonder, can the church evolve in such a way that Christ truly becomes the center of this universe, the center of different cultures, religions, genders, and peoples? How can we evolve to a new consciousness of relatedness where justice and peace rule the human heart? Is it possible to evolve to an ultrahumanism, a deepening of organic life, or are we as a planet simply on a downward spiral toward annihilation of all that gives meaning and purpose to life?

The human heart is made for God and can find rest only in God. That is why, despite the gloomy picture of Friedman's hot, flat, and crowded earth, something new is germinating in our midst. There are new groups, small communities of men and women committed to holistic life: simple living, tilling the soil, healthy eating, and caring for one another and for the poor. I call these nascent communities *Christ seeds.* They are morphogenetic fields of gospel life appearing all over, under many different names, yet expressing gospel values: unity, healing of the earth, wholeness of relationships, and peace. In a sense they are truly *catholic,* irrespective of their members' personal religious commitment. They are the evolvers in our midst willing to sacrifice personal gain, seeking to make wholes by making their own lives whole through a balance of spiritual, bodily, and material energies that extends to the earth and to community.

But I also see a distinct role for Christians in this process of evolution. We who are baptized into cosmic evolution have a responsibility to evolve and to help this creation evolve toward unity in love. On the whole, Christians do not have a consciousness of evolution, nor do Christians see Christ as the future of evolution. Yet because we are baptized into Christ we have accepted the task of becoming a new creation and joining all creation in this new life of Christ. It is time, therefore, to put aside our differences and to engage evolution as the birth of Christ within. If God is absent from the world, maybe it is because we refuse to give birth to God in our daily lives; we refuse to incarnate the Word, to make God come alive. Christ is not an abstract thought but the living Word of God who lives in the heart of the world and in human hearts. A privatized faith rejects the demands of an incarnate God. When faith turns religious practice on to autopilot, it becomes mechanized, programmed into a mindless routine, a "faceless faith" uttering prayers while the heart is far from God. Such mechanized faith makes possible a hot, flat, and crowded earth because without enfleshing the Word of God we are unable to see the flesh of God. To see another and not respond is like looking into a mirror and not recognizing ourself. The human face demands an ethical response. We act for others when we know ourselves to be related to others.

The emergence of Christ depends on our capacity to love, to become whole-makers. The love of God is poured out into our hearts through the Holy Spirit, and it is always new. The Spirit is the dynamic newness of love that draws us into unity, into relationships that demand our conscious participation. Whether we see the present moment as hopeful or hopeless, it is our moment to act. We need to let go of controlling God, controlling our lives, controlling the church, and controlling the world. All is gift, and our human role is to receive the gift of life in all its diversity and to respond graciously. The God of evolution is the God of adventure, a God who loves to do new things and is always new. We are invited into this adventure of love to find our freedom in love and to love without measure.

Notes

Introduction

1. Pierre Teilhard de Chardin, *Christianity and Evolution*, trans. René Hague (New York: Harcourt Brace and Co., 1969), 87.

2. John F. Haught, *God after Darwin: A Theology of Evolution* (Boulder, CO: Westview Press, 2000), 5.

3. Erich Jantsch, quoted in Margaret Wheatley, *Leadership and the New Science: Discovering Order in a Chaotic World* (Berkeley, CA: Berrett Koehler, 1994), 74.

4. Pierre Teilhard de Chardin, *The Divine Milieu: An Essay on the Interior Life*, trans. William Collins (New York: Harper and Row, 1969), 68–69.

5. See Barbara Fiand, *Releasement: Spirituality for Ministry* (New York: Crossroad, 1987), 39.

6. Nicolas Berdyaev, *The Destiny of Man* (New York: Harper Torch books, 1960), 28.

7. Sean Edward Kinsella, "How Great a Gladness: Some Thoughts on Francis of Assisi and the Natural World," *Studies in Spirituality* 12 (2002): 66.

8. Roger D. Sorrell, *St. Francis of Assisi and Nature: Tradition and Innovation in Western Christian Attitudes toward the Environment* (New York: Oxford University Press, 1988), 89; Ewert Cousins, "Francis of Assisi: Christian Mysticism at the Crossroads," in *Mysticism and Religious Traditions*, ed. S. Katz (New York: Oxford, 1983), 165.

9. Teilhard de Chardin, *Christianity and Evolution*, 239.

10. John Haughey, SJ, *Where Is Knowing Going? The Horizons of the Knowing Subject* (Washington, DC: Georgetown University Press, 2009), 40, 45.

11. Ibid., 49.

12. John F. Haught, *Deeper than Darwin* (Boulder, CO: Westview Press, 2003), 164.

13. Teilhard de Chardin, *Christianity and Evolution*, 240.

14. Haught, *Deeper than Darwin*, 164.

15. See Eckhart Tolle, *The Power of Now: A Guide to Spiritual Enlightenment* (Novato, CA: New World Library, 2004). The basic message of Tolle's book is that our mode of consciousness can be transformed by becoming free of the egoic mind, with all its consequences, to become deeply conscious of this present moment, or, as Tolle often calls it, "the now."

16. For a discussion on first and second axial periods, see Ewert H. Cousins, *Christ of the Twenty-first Century* (Rockport, MA: Element Books, 1992), 7–10; Ilia Delio, *Christ in Evolution* (Maryknoll, NY: Orbis Books, 2008), 23–29.

17. Karl Rahner, quoted in Catherine LaCugna, *God for Us: The Trinity and Christian Life* (San Francisco, CA: HarperSan Francisco, 1993), 6.

Chapter 1. The Book of Creation

1. Adam Frank, *The Constant Fire: Beyond the Science vs. Religion Debate* (Berkeley and Los Angeles: University of California Press, 2009), 146. See also Simon Singh, *Big Bang: The Origin of the Universe* (New York: HarperCollins, 2004), 120–28. For a succinct description of the new cosmology, see Brian Swimme and Thomas Berry, *The Universe Story: From the Primordial Flaring Forth to the Ecozoic Era—A Celebration of the Unfolding of the Cosmos* (New York: HarperOne, 1994); Judy Cannato, *Radical Amazement: Contemplative Lessons from Black Holes, Supernovas, and Other Wonders of the Universe* (Notre Dame, IN: Sorin Books, 2006).

2. Frank, *The Constant Fire*, 147.

3. Ibid., 149; see also Singh, *Big Bang*, 214–29.

4. Frank, *The Constant Fire*, 149.

5. Ibid., 149.

6. Ibid., 150; see also Singh, *Big Bang*, 422–37.

7. Frank, *The Constant Fire*, 152–55.

8. For a discussion on strong and weak versions of the anthropic principle, see John F. Haught, *Science and Religion: From Conflict to Conversation* (Mahwah, NJ: Paulist Press, 1995), 120–41.

9. Cannato, *Radical Amazement*, 42.

10. Francisco J. Ayala, "Biological Evolution: An Introduction," in *An Evolving Dialogue: Theological and Scientific Perspectives on Evolution*, ed. James Miller (Harrisburg, PA: Trinity Press International, 2001), 13.

11. Barbara Taylor Brown, *The Luminous Web* (Cambridge, MA: Cowley Publications, 2000), 25.

12. Daniel Dennett, quoted in John F. Haught, *God after Darwin: A Theology of Evolution* (Boulder, CO: Westview Press, 2000), 11.

13. Haught, *God after Darwin*, 5.

14. John F. Haught, *Making Sense of Evolution: Darwin, God, and the Drama of Life* (Louisville, KY: Westminster John Knox Press, 2010), xiii.

15. Haught, *God after Darwin*, 40.

16. Prior to Darwin, Jean-Baptiste Lamarck posited ideas on the inheritance of acquired characteristics and the use and disuse of organs in view of evolution. One of his principal insights, based on environmental factors, is that form follows function. See http://www.serpentfd.org/b/lamarck.html.

17. John Haught, *Is Nature Enough? Meaning and Truth in the Age of Science* (New York: Cambridge University Press, 2006), 57–58.

18. Denis Edwards, *Ecology at the Heart of Faith: The Change of the Heart that Leads to a New Way of Living on Earth* (Maryknoll, NY: Orbis Books, 2008), 12–13.

19. William Grassie, "The Evolution of Religion: Memes, Spandrels, or Adaptation?" Lecture presented at the Society for the Integration of Science and Human Values Department of Pali and Buddhist Studies, the University of Peradeniya, Kandy, Sri Lanka, November 1, 2007. Available on the www.grassie.net website.

20. See Pierre Teilhard de Chardin, *Activation of Energy*, trans. René Hague (New York: Harcourt Brace Jovanovich, 1970), 387–403; idem, *The Phenomenon of Man*, trans. Bernard Wall (New York: Harper and Row, 1959), 46–66. For a good discussion on the origin of Homo sapiens, see also Diarmuid O'Murchu, *Ancestral Grace: Meeting God in Our Human Story* (Maryknoll, NY: Orbis Books, 2008), 36–71.

21. Pierre Teilhard de Chardin, *Christianity and Evolution*, trans. René Hague (New York: Harcourt Brace and Co., 1969), 87.

22. Philip Clayton, "Neuroscience, the Person, and God: An Emergentist Account," in *Neuroscience and the Person: Scientific Perspectives on Divine Action*, ed. Robert John Russell, Nancey Murphy, Theo C. Meyering, and Michael A. Arbib (Vatican City: Vatican Observatory; Berkeley, CA: Center for Theology and the Natural Sciences, 1999), 211.

23. Philip Clayton, "Emerging God." Available on the www.religion-online.org website.

24. Teilhard, *Christianity and Evolution*, 221.

25. Ibid., 84.

26. John F. Haught, *Responses to 101 Questions on God and Evolution* (Mahwah, NJ: Paulist Press, 2001).

27. Ibid., 7.

28. Michael Specter, "A Life of Its Own: Where Will Synthetic Biology Lead Us?" *The New Yorker* (September 28, 2009): 65.

29. http://www.gallup.com/poll/114544/Darwin-Birthday-Believe-Evolution.aspx. According to the poll, 39 percent of the public accepted

evolution, 25 percent rejected evolution, and 36 percent did not have an opinion one way or another.

30. Pope John Paul II, "Address of Pope John Paul II to the Pontifical Academy of Sciences," October 22, 1996. The pope's statement on dialogue between the church and science reiterates a statement he made in a previous address to scientists. See Pope John Paul II, "Discourse to the Academy of Sciences," October 28, 1986, no. 1.

31. John Paul II, "Address of Pope John Paul II to the Pontifical Academy of Sciences." The pope continued: "Rather than speaking about the theory of evolution, it is more accurate to speak of the theories of evolution. The use of the plural is required here—in part because of the diversity of explanations regarding the mechanism of evolution, and in part because of the diversity of philosophies involved" (no. 4); cf. Francis S. Collins, *The Language of God: A Scientist Presents Evidence for Belief* (New York: Free Press, 2006), 202.

32. According to John Haught: "All theists accept the doctrine of creation, but the term 'creationism' usually refers to the beliefs of biblical literalists who reject evolutionary biology. There are several kinds of creationists. 'Young earth' creationists hold that about 6,000 years ago God made the universe in six literal calendar days of the week as depicted in Genesis 1:1–2:3. . . . 'Old earth' creationists are more open to current scientific depictions of earth-history as being 4.5 billion years long. However, like other creationists they claim that the various kinds of life could not have been created by natural processes from inanimate stuff, but only by God's 'special creation'" (*Responses to 101 Questions on God and Evolution*, 71–82).

33. Archbishop Gianfranco Ravasi, quoted in "Evolutionay Theory Not "Incompatible" with Catholicism, Vatican Official Says," Catholic News Agency, Vatican City, September 17, 2008 (available on the catholicnewsagency.com website). According to several news reports on the Vatican-sponsored conferred on evolution, Archbishop Ravasi claimed that Darwin's theory of evolution could even be traced to Saint Augustine and Saint Thomas Aquinas.

34. Marc Leclerc, quoted in John Allen, "Genesis Isn't a Science Book: Vatican to Study Evolution; Benedict's Trip to France; and Pius XII," *National Catholic Reporter* (September 19, 2008). Intelligent design theorists posit irreducible complexity in nature that cannot be explained by evolution alone; hence, some type of informational source outside the cosmic process is responsible for complex order within the process. See Haught, *Is Nature Enough?* 67–69.

35. Niels Bohr, quoted in John Gribbin, *In Search of Schrödinger's Cat* (Toronto: Bantam Books, 1984), 5; Singh, *Big Bang*, 492.

36. For a discussion on the double-slit experiment, see Jack Geis, *Physics, Metaphysics, and God* (Bloomington, IN: AuthorHouse, 2003); Shan Gao, *God Does Play Dice with the Universe* (Suffolk: Abramis, 2008).

37. Brian Greene, *The Fabric of the Cosmos: Space, Time, and the Texture of Reality* (New York: Vintage Books, 2004), 206.

38. Gribbin, *In Search of Schrödinger's Cat*, 171.

39. Niels Bohr, quoted in Gribbin, *In Search of Schrödinger's Cat*, 184.

40. See Fritjof Capra, *The Web of Life: A New Scientific Understanding of Living Systems* (New York: Doubleday, 1996), 36–50.

41. Ludwig von Bertalanffy, cited in Capra, *Web of Life*, 47.

42. For a discussion on systems theories, see Capra, *The Web of Life*, 36–50.

43. Ibid., 48.

44. Margaret Wheatley, *Leadership and the New Science: Learning about Organization from an Orderly Universe* (San Francisco: Berrett-Koehler, 1992), 121–27.

45. Brian Swimme, *The Universe Is a Green Dragon: A Cosmic Creation Story* (Santa Fe, NM: Bear and Company, 1984), 32.

46. A. Einstein, B. Podolsky, and N. Rosen, "Can Quantum Mechanical Description of Physical Reality Be Considered Complete?" *Physical Review* 47 (May 15, 1935): 777–80.

47. Erwin Schrödinger, in "The Present Situation in Quantum Mechanics: A Translation of Schödinger's 'Cat Paradox' Paper," trans. John D. Trimmer, *Proceedings of the American Philosophical Society* 124. Available online.

48. Arthur Fine, "The Einstein-Podolsky-Rosen Argument in Quantum Theory." Available online.

49. Kevin J. Sharpe, "Relating the Physics and Metaphysics of David Bohm," *Zygon: Journal of Religion and Science* 25, no. 1 (March 1990): 105–22. Available on the ksharpe.com website.

50. Ibid.

51. Ibid.

52. For a discussion of holons, see Cannato, *Radical Amazement*, 94–102; Judy Cannato, *Fields of Compassion: How the New Cosmology Is Transforming Spiritual Life* (Notre Dame, IN: Sorin Books, 2010); Ken Wilber, *A Theory of Everything* (Boston: Shambhala Publications, 2000), 27–39.

53. Mark Edwards, "A Brief History of Holons" (2003). Available online.

54. Wilber, *A Theory of Everything*, 50.

55. Ken Wilber, *Sex, Ecology, Spirituality: The Spirit of Evolution* (Boston: Shambhala Publications, 2001), 43–85.

56. Rupert Sheldrake, *The Presence of the Past: Morphic Resonance and the Habits of Nature* (London: Willaim Collins Sons, 1988), 189–90.

57. Cannato, *Radical Amazement*, 84–90; Cannato, *Fields of Compassion*, 25–32.

58. This is Saint Augustine's doctrine of *rationes seminales*, which was influential on Bonaventure "[Latin, from the Greek *logoi spermatikoi*, germinal principles or original factors]" (brackets in original) was "a notion employed by the Stoics, Neoplatonists, and Augustine. It is usually translated as seminal reason or seminal virtue. By this term Augustine meant the seeds, potential powers, or causes of the subsequent developments in the physical order after God's creation. Change is simply the realization of what already exists virtually. These seeds were themselves created by God when God created the world. This view was intended to reconcile the tension between the belief that God created all things and the evident fact that new things are constantly developing for according to this view, the development of every new thing is simply the unfolding of what has been in the world from the beginning" ("Rationes Seminales," available on the blackwellreference website; see also Haught, *Making Sense of Evolution*, 42).

59. Postmodern philosophy grapples with an understanding of being, especially in light of the new science. The de-ontologizing of God has revealed mystery at the heart of the universe, as Jean Luc Marion described in *God without Being*, trans. Thomas Carlson (Chicago: University of Chicago Press, 1995). Commenting on postmodernity and epistemology, philosopher John Deely writes: "The postmodern era is positioned to synthesize at a higher level—the level of experience, where the being of things and the activity of the finite knower compenetrate one another and provide the materials whence can be derived knowledge of nature and knowledge of culture in their full symbiosis" ("Philosophy and Experience," *American Catholic Philosophical Quarterly* 66, no. 4 [Winter 1992], 314–15.

Chapter 2. The Evolution of God

1. Thomas Aquinas, *Summa Contra Gentiles* II.2.3.

2. Cyprian Smith, cited in John Shea, *Following Jesus* (Maryknoll, NY: Orbis Books, 2010), 60–61.

3. Fritjof Capra, *The Tao of Physics* (New York: Bantam Books, 1984), 117–275.

4. John F. Haught, *Responses to 101 Questions on God and Evolution* (Mahwah, NJ: Paulist Press, 2001), 136.

5. Joseph A. Bracken, *Subjectivity, Objectivity, and Intersubjectivity* (West Conshohocken, PA: Templeton Foundation Press, 2009), 173.

6. Pierre Teilhard de Chardin, *Christianity and Evolution*, trans. René Hague (New York: Harcourt Brace and Co., 1969), 240.

7. Ibid., 239.

8. Ibid., 26.

9. See Denis Edwards, *How God Acts: Creation, Redemption, and Special Divine Action* (Minneapolis: Fortress Press, 2010), 47.

10. Bernard McGinn, "The Dynamism of the Trinity in Bonaventure and Meister Eckhart," *Franciscan Studies* 65 (2007): 142.

11. Bonaventure I *Sentence* (*Sent.*) d. 27, p.1, a.un., q.2, ad 3 (I, 470). The idea that the Father is innascible (self-existent) and fecund underlies the dialectical style of Bonaventure's thought. It also provides the basis of Bonaventure's metaphysics as a *coincidentia oppositorum*. The Father's innascibility and fecundity are mutually complementary opposites; they cannot be formally reduced to one or the other; the Father is generative precisely because he is unbegotten. See Zachary Hayes, "Introduction," in *Disputed Questions on the Mystery of the Trinity*, vol. 3, *Works of Saint Bonaventure*, ed. George Marcil (New York: The Franciscan Institute, 1979), 42n.51.

12. Bonaventure I *Sent.* d. 5, a. 1, q. 2, resp. (I, 115), I *Sent.* d. 2, a.u., q. 4, fund 2 (I, 56); Hayes, introduction, 34, n. 10. Bonaventure uses the terms *per modum naturae* and *per modum voluntatis* to designate the two trinitarian emanations. The terms are inspired by Aristotle's principle that there exist only two perfect modes of production, namely, natural and free.

13. Bonaventure I *Sent.* d. 6, a.u., q. 2, resp. (I, 128). 'Processus per modum voluntatis concomitante natura'; Kevin P. Keane, "Why Creation? Bonaventure and Thomas Aquinas on God as Creative Good," *Downside Review* 93 (1975): 15. Keane writes: "It is noteworthy that Bonaventure's reason for attributing creation to the divine will is quite different from Thomas's. Where Thomas is in the main concerned to protect the divine perfection and radically free will, Bonaventure is at pains to elucidate how only through the will can an act be truly personal—both free and expressive of the outward dynamism of goodness, an act spontaneous yet substantial."

14. Bonaventure shows a decided preference for the term *Word*; this title signifies a complex network of relations that the Son bears to the Father, to creation, to humanity, and to revelation. See Zachary Hayes, "The Meaning of *Convenientia* in the Metaphysics of St. Bonaventure," *Franciscan Studies* 34 (1974): 90.

15. Zachary Hayes, "Christology and Metaphysics in the Thought of Bonaventure," *Journal of Religion* (Supplement, 1978): S91.

16. Ibid.," S88–S92.

17. Bonaventure, in Hayes, "Meaning of *Convenientia* in the Metaphysics of St. Bonaventure," 99.

18. Emmanuel Falque, "The Phenomenological Act of *Perscrutatio* in the Proemium of St. Bonaventure's Commentary on the Sentences," trans. Elisa Mangina, *Medieval Philosophy and Theology* 10 (2001): 18.

19. For similarities and differences between the trinitarian theologies of Bonaventure and Eckhart, see McGinn, "The Dynamism of the Trinity in Bonaventure and Meister Eckhart," 147–55. McGinn identifies three differences: (1) the transcendental predicate *bonum/bonitas* plays a more limited role in Eckhart than it does in Bonaventure, (2) Eckhart, more so than Bonaventure, links the emanation of the universe from God with the inner procession of the persons in the Trinity, and (3) while the ultimate unknowability of God is important for Bonaventure, Eckhart's teaching about God is more apophatic.

20. Meister Eckhart, *Sermo* 53. Trans. Edmund Colledge, OSA, and Bernard McGinn, *Meister Eckhart: The Essential Sermons, Commentaries, Treatises, and Defense* (New York: Paulist Press, 1981), 205.

21. McGinn, "Introduction," *Meister Eckhart*, 41. Eckhart's teaching on the eternity of creation has a subtle distinction between creation as eternal in itself and as an overflow of God's being. Creation is *ex nihilo* insofar as it has no other source but God; however, it is eternal insofar as God is eternal. It is constantly new because "the Word is always being born and the created thing is always coming to be" (*Sermon* 15.2).

22. McGinn, "Introduction," 37.

23. Ibid., 38.

24. McGinn notes that "the Dominican differs from the Franciscan in his stress on a pure and hidden potentiality, the inner ground or desert, unmoved in itself, but the necessary precondition of all emanation in God and in creation. This ground is the Father in one sense, but not in another" ("The Dynamism of the Trinity in Bonaventure and Meister Eckhart," 153).

25. Denis Edwards, *The God of Evolution* (New York: Paulist Press, 1999), 31.

26. We can draw a parallel here between the singularity of the Father and the singularity of the universe, which is a hypothetical point of zero volume containing infinite mass. The singularity essentially marks the Big Bang and hence the beginning of evolution.

27. Joseph Bracken, *The Divine Matrix: Creativity as Link between East and West* (Maryknoll, NY: Orbis Books, 1995), 65. Bracken interprets Whitehead's dynamic trinitarian scheme as the basis of creativity, which is an ongoing activity constitutive of the divine persons and of all their creatures in the extensive continuum.

28. Matthew Fox, trans., *Meditations with Meister Eckhart* (Santa Fe, NM: Bear and Company, 1983), 32.

29. David A. Cooper, *God Is a Verb: Kabbalah and the Practice of Mystical Judaism* (New York: Riverhead Books, 1997), 70.

30. Karl Rahner, "Evolution," in *Sacramentum Mundi: Volume Two*, ed. Karl Rahner, Cornelius Ernst, and Kevin Smyth, 289–97 (London: Burns and Oates, 1968), quoted in Denis Edwards, *Breath of Life: A Theology of the Creator Spirit* (Maryknoll, NY: Orbis Books, 2004), 46.

31. Ibid.

32. Ibid.

33. Wolfhart Pannenberg, cited in Edwards, *Breath of Life*, 113, 138; see also Edwards, "A Relational and Evolving Universe," 208.

34. Teilhard de Chardin, *Christianity and Evolution*, 240.

35. John F. Haught, *Deeper Than Darwin* (Boulder, CO: Westview Press, 2003), 174.

Chapter 3. Creative Union

1. Dogmatic decree, Fourth General Council, fifth session, October 22, AD 450, Chalcedon, Bithynia, Asia Minor. Widely available on the Internet.

2. F. LeRon Shults, *Christology and Science* (Grand Rapids, MI: Eerdmans, 2008), 43.

3. Pierre Teilhard de Chardin, *Christianity and Evolution*, trans. René Hague (New York: Harcourt Brace and Co., 1969), 26.

4. Christopher Mooney, SJ, *Teilhard de Chardin and the Mystery of Christ* (New York: Harper and Row, 1966), 174–75.

5. Teilhard de Chardin, *Christianity and Evolution*, 157.

6. Ibid., 62.

7. Ursula King, "Introduction," in *Pierre Teilhard de Chardin: Writings/Selected* (Maryknoll, NY: Orbis Books, 1999), 62.

8. Pierre Teilhard de Chardin, *Activation of Energy*, trans. René Hague (New York: Harcourt Brace Jovanovich, 1971), 262.

9. Ibid., 263.

10. See Phillippe Yates, "The Primacy of Christ in John Duns Scotus: An Assessment," *FAITH Magazine* (January-February 2008); available online. See also Ilia Delio, *A Franciscan View of Creation: Learning to Live in a Sacramental World*, ed. Elise Saggau, vol. 2, *The Franciscan Heritage Series*, ed. Joseph P. Chinnici (New York: The Franciscan Institute, 2003), 39.

11. In his introduction to Teilhard's *Christianity and Evolution*, Max Wildiers states that Teilhard diverges from Scotus on a number of

important points. Scotus, Wildiers writes, "takes God as his starting point and asks what was the divine intention in decreeing the incarnation of the Word. Teilhard considers the value of the world and asks how it can be related to the incarnate Word." Scotus is more interested in the pre-existence of Christ in relation to the future creation, whereas Teilhard emphasized eschatology and Christ as the final consecration of the earth. For Scotus, Christ is first in the divine intention of creation; for Teilhard, Christ is the culmination of history (*Christianity and Evolution*, 12). Although Wildiers points are interesting, a more critical study of Scotus and Teilhard may reveal more similarities than differences.

12. Beatrice Bruteau, *Evolution toward Divinity: Teilhard de Chardin and the Hindu Traditions* (Wheaton, IL: The Theosophical Publishing House, 1974), 7.

13. Pierre Teilhard de Chardin, *Letters from a Traveler* (New York: Harper and Row, 1962), 324n.1, quoted in Bruteau, *Evolution toward Divinity*, 21.

14. Teilhard de Chardin, *Christianity and Evolution*, 181.

15. Ibid., 89.

16. Ibid., 91–92.

17. Ibid., 181.

18. *Pierre Teilhard de Chardin*, 94.

19. Pierre Teilhard de Chardin, "My Universe," in *Process Theology: Basic Writings*, ed. Evert H. Cousins (New York: Newman Press, 1971), 254.

20. Pierre Teilhard de Chardin, *The Phenomenon of Man*, trans. Bernard Wall (New York: Harper and Row, 1959), 293–94; Timothy Jamison, "The Personalized Universe of Teilhard de Chardin," in *There Shall Be One Christ*, ed. Michael Meilach (New York: The Franciscan Institute, 1968), 26.

21. Teilhard de Chardin, *Phenomenon of Man*, 53–56.

22. Teilhard de Chardin, *Christianity and Evolution*, 171.

23. Karl Rahner, "The Specific Character of the Christian Concept of God," in *Theological Investigations* (New York: Crossroad, 1988), 21:185–95.

24. Ibid., 191.

25. Teilhard de Chardin, *Christianity and Evolution*, 176–77.

26. Ibid., 177.

27. Ibid., 178.

28. Ibid.

29. Ibid., 179.

30. Ibid., 184.

31. Ibid., 179.

32. Ibid., 182.

33. John F. Haught, *Deeper than Darwin* (Boulder, CO: Westview Press, 2003), 174.

34. Niels Henrik Gregersen, "Emergence and Complexity," in *The Oxford Handbook of Religion and Science*, ed. Philip Clayton and Zachary Simpson (New York: Oxford University Press, 2006), 767.

35. Philip Clayton, "Neuroscience, the Person, and God: An Emergentist Account," in *Neuroscience and the Person: Scientific Perspectives on Divine Action*, ed. Robert John Russell, Nancey Murphy, Theo C. Meyering, and Michael A. Arbib (Vatican City: Vatican Observatory; Berkeley, CA: Center for Theology and the Natural Sciences, 1999), 211.

36. Philip Clayton, *Mind and Emergence: From Quantum to Consciousness* (New York: Oxford University Press, 2004), 39.

37. Denis Edwards, *Breath of Life: A Theology of the Creator Spirit* (Maryknoll, NY: Orbis Books, 2004), 136.

38. Gregersen, "Emergence and Complexity," 767.

39. Denis Edwards, *Jesus and the Cosmos* (New York: Paulist Press, 1991), 66.

40. William M. Thompson, *Christ and Consciousness: Exploring Christ's Contribution to Human Consciousness: The Origins and Development of Christian Consciousness* (New York: Paulist Press, 1977), 63, 65.

41. Ibid., 67.

42. John B. Cobb, *The Structure of Christian Existence* (New York: Seabury Press, 1979), 122.

43. Shults, *Christology and Science*, 43.

44. Ibid.

45. Jane Kopas, *Sacred Identity: Exploring a Theology of Person* (New York: Paulist Press, 1994), 178.

46. Ibid.

47. See Adriaan Theodoor Peperzak, *Beyond: The Philosophy of Emmanuel Levinas* (Evanston, IL: Northwestern University Press, 1997), 175; Robyn Horner, *Rethinking God as Gift: Marion, Derrida, and the Limits of Phenomenology* (New York: Fordham, 2001), 64–66.

48. John F. Haught, "Theology and Ecology in an Unfinished Universe," in *Franciscans and Creation: What Is Our Responsibility?* ed. Elise Saggau (New York: The Franciscan Institute, 2003), 9.

49. See Zachary Hayes, "Christ, the Word of God and Exemplar of Humanity," *Cord* 46, no. 1 (1996): 9.

Chapter 4. Jesus the Whole-Maker

1. Ignatius of Antioch, "The Epistle of St. Ignatius of Antioch to the of Smyrnaeans," 8:2, trans. Charles Hoole; available online.

2. John Haughey, SJ, *Where Is Knowing Going? The Horizons of the Knowing Subject* (Washington, DC: Georgetown University Press, 2009), 40.

3. Walter J. Ong, "Yeast: A Parable for Catholic Higher Education," *America* (April 7, 1990): 347.

4. Ignatius of Antioch, "The Epistle of St. Ignatius of Antioch to the of Smyrnaeans," 8:2.

5. Michael W. Holmes, trans., "The Martyrdom of Polycarp," para. 19, in *The Apostolic Fathers*, rev. ed., 226–45 (Grand Rapids, MI: Baker Books, 1999), 243.

6. Holmes, *The Apostolic Fathers*, 261.

7. Cyril of Jerusalem, "Catechetical Discourses," trans. Charles Hoole, sect. 23; available online.

8. J. N. D. Kelly, *Early Christian Doctrines* (New York: Harper and Row, 1978), 190–1.

9. Mark Hathaway and Leonardo Boff, *The Tao of Liberation: Exploring the Ecology of Transformation* (Maryknoll, NY: Orbis Books, 2009), 331.

10. Ong, "Yeast," 347.

11. Ibid., 348.

12. Wolfart Pannenberg views the kingdom present only in expectation evoked from proclamation rather than materially present in Christ's person and/or in a penultimate sense. The absence of God in the present, according to Pannenberg, is the negative side of God's futurity. "In Jesus' message it is only *as future that God is present*." See Wolfart Pannenberg, *Theology and the Kingdom of God*, ed. Richard John Neuhaus (Philadelphia: Westminster Press, 1977), 68.

13. Arthur Peacocke, "Nature as Sacrament," Keene Lecture 2, November 21, 2001; available online.

14. Dietrich Bonhoeffer, *Letters and Papers from Prison*, ed. Eberhard Bethge, trans. Reginald Fuller et al. (New York: Macmillan, 1971), 17.

15. Miroslav Volf, *Exclusion and Embrace: A Theological Exploration of Identity Otherness, and Reconciliation* (Nashville, TN: Abingdon Press, 1996), 47.

16. N. Max Wildiers, *The Theologian and His Universe: Theology and Cosmology from the Middle Ages to the Present* (New York: Seabury Press, 1982), 222.

17. Albert Haase, *Swimming in the Sun: Discovering the Lord's Prayer with Francis of Assisi and Thomas Merton* (Cincinnati: St. Anthony Messenger Press, 1993), 144.

18. Volf, *Exclusion and Embrace*, 129.

19. Ibid., 127.

20. Ibid., 126.

21. Ibid., 129.

22. Ibid.

23. John Zizioulas, *Being as Communion: Studies in Personhood and the Church* (Crestwood, NY: St. Vladimir's Seminary Press, 1985), 58.

24. Volf, *Exclusion and Embrace*, 130.

25. Denis Edwards, *Jesus and the Cosmos* (New York: Paulist Press, 1991), 66.

26. Ilia Delio, *Christ in Evolution* (Maryknoll, NY: Orbis Books, 2008), 39, 110, 128.

27. Edwards, *Jesus and the Cosmos*, 93.

28. Pierre Teilhard de Chardin, *The Future of Man*, trans. Norman Denny (New York: Harper and Row, 1964), 309. In the last entry in his journal, made three days before his death on Easter Sunday 1955, Teilhard brought together his principal thesis: *"Noogenesis=Christogenesis (=Paul)"* summed up in Paul's First Letter to the Corinthians (15:28): "that God may be all in all" (*En pasi panta Theos*).

29. Isaac of Stella, cited in Caroline Walker Bynum, *Jesus as Mother: Studies in the Spirituality of the High Middle Ages* (Berkeley and Los Angeles: University of California Press, 1982), 95.

Chapter 5. Resurrection and Transformation

1. N. T. Wright, "Early Traditions and the Origin of Christianity," *Sewanee Theological Review* 41.2 (1998); available online.

2. N. T. Wright, *Surprised by Hope: Rethinking Heaven, the Resurrection, and the Mission of the Church* (New York: HarperOne, 2008), 67.

3. John Dominic Crossan, "The Resurrection of Jesus in Its Jewish Context," *Neotestamentica* 37, no. 1 (2003): 42–43.

4. Robert B. Stewart, ed., *The Resurrection of Jesus: John Dominic Crossan and N. T. Wright in Dialogue* (Minneapolis: Fortress Press, 2006), 25.

5. Wright, *Surprised by Hope*, 46.

6. Ibid., 42.

7. Ibid., 111.

8. John Shea, *Following Jesus* (Maryknoll, NY: Orbis Books, 2010), 61. Shea writes: "Heaven is an image for a higher consciousness. When we are aware that our origin and destiny is God and, right here and now, the generative love of God who is called Father has given everything into our hands, we are 'in heaven.' Heaven is within."

9. See, for example, Francis of Assisi, "A Prayer Inspired by the Our Father," in which he writes: "O Our Father most holy: Creator, Redeemer, Consoler, and Savior: Who are in heaven: In the angels and the saints, enlightening them to know, for You, Lord, are light; inflaming them to love, for You, Lord, are love; dwelling in them and filling them with happiness." In *Francis of Assisi: Early Documents*, vol. 1, *The Saint*, ed. Regis J. Armstrong, J. A. Wayne Hellmann, and William J. Short (New York: New City Press, 1999), 158.

10. Jürgen Moltmann, *God in Creation: A New Theology of Creation and the Spirit of God*, trans. Margaret Kohl (Minneapolis: Fortress Press, 1993), 165, 167.

11. Bishop N. T. Wright, "On Earth As in Heaven: Acts 16.16–34; John 17.20–end." A sermon at the Eucharist on the Sunday after Ascension Day, May 20, 2007, York Minster, England; available online.

12. Karl Rahner, quoted in Denis Edwards, "Resurrection and the Costs of Evolution: A Dialogue with Rahner on Noninterventionist Theology," *Theological Studies* 67 (2006): 823.

13. Bonaventure, *Sermo* IX, cited in Zachary Hayes, "Christ, Word of God and Exemplar of Humanity," *Cord* 46, no. 1 (1996): 13.

14. Judy Cannato, *Radical Amazement: Contemplative Lessons from Black Holes, Supernovas, and Other Wonders of the Universe* (Notre Dame, IN: Sorin Books, 2006), 119–20.

15. Holmes Rolston, III, "Kenosis and Nature," in *The Work of Love: Creation as Kenosis*, ed. John Polkinghorne (Grand Rapids, MI: Eerdmans, 2001), 59–60.

16. Annie Dillard, *Pilgrim at Tinker Creek* (New York: Harper's Magazine Press, 1974), 144.

17. Ibid., 67–68.

18. Alfred Kracher, "The Diversity of Environments: Nature and Technology as Competing Myths," in *Creation's Diversity: Voices of Theology and Science*, ed. Willem B. Drees et al. (London: T&T Clark, 2008), 84.

19. Ibid.

20. Pierre Teilhard de Chardin, "Comment je vois," in Georges Crespy, *From Science to Theology: An Essay on Teilhard de Chardin*, trans. George H. Shriver (New York: Abingdon Press, 1968), 99.

21. Ibid.

22. Ibid.

23. Gloria Schwab, "The Creative Suffering of the Triune God: An Evolutionary Pantheistic Paradigm," *Theology and Science* 5, no. 3 (2007): 293.

24. Descartes, in *The Philosophical Works of Descartes*, vol. 1, trans. Elizabeth S. Haldane and G. R. T. Ross (New York: Cambridge University Press, 1970), 101, cited in Antonio D'Amasio, *Descartes' Error: Emotion, Reason, and the Human Brain* (New York: Penguin, 2005), 249.

25. Heidi Russell, "Quantum Analogy: Rethinking the Human Person as Spirit/Body," paper presented at the Sixty-Fourth Annual Conference of the *Catholic Theological Society of America*, Halifax, Nova Scotia, June 2009, p. 6.

26. Ibid.

27. Mark Graves, *Mind, Brain, and the Elusive Soul* (Burlington, VT: Ashgate, 2008), 206.

28. D'Amasio, *Descartes' Error,* xvi.

29. Rupert Sheldrake, *The Presence of the Past: Morphic Resonance and the Habits of Nature* (Rochester, VT: Park Street Press, 1995), 65.

30. See William Hasker, *The Emergent Self* (Ithaca, NY: Cornell University Press, 1999), 147–61.

31. Ibid., 161–70.

32. Alfred North Whitehead, quoted in Joseph A. Bracken, "Bodily Resurrection and the Dialectic of Spirit and Matter," *Theological Studies* 66 (2005): 776.

33. Bracken, "Bodily Resurrection," 778.

34. Ibid., 774.

35. Joseph A. Bracken, *Subjectivity, Objectivity, and Intersubjectivity: A New Paradigm for Religion and Science* (Conshohoken, PA: Templeton Press, 2009), 161.

36. Alfred North Whitehead, *Process and Reality*, ed. David Ray Griffin and Donald W. Sherburne (New York: Free Press, 1978), 29.

37. Teilhard de Chardin, *The Phenomenon of Man*, trans. Bernard Wall (New York: Harper and Row, 1959), 53–66.

38. Bracken, *Subjectivity, Objectivity, and Intersubjectivity*, 160.

39. Alfred North Whitehead, quoted in Bracken, *Subjectivity, Objectivity, and Intersubjectivity*, 171.

40. Bracken, *Subjectivity, Objectivity, and Intersubjectivity*, 172.

41. Ibid.

42. The Latin term *haecceitas* was used by the medieval Franciscan theologian John Duns Scotus to describe individuation of being. On the use of the term *haecceitas*, see Allan Wolter, "Scotus's Individuation Theory," in *The Philosophical Theology of John Duns Scotus*, ed. Marilyn McCord Adams (Ithaca, NY: Cornell University Press, 1990), 76n.26,; ibid., *Duns Scotus' Early Oxford Lecture on Individuation* (Santa Barbara, CA: Old Mission, 1992).

43. Edwards, "Resurrection and the Costs of Evolution," 816.

44. The term "theandric" is borrowed from the fifth-century theologian Maximus the Confessor, who described the divine-created union of energies of Jesus Christ as "theandric." See also David Coffey, "The Theandric Nature of Christ," *Theological Studies* 60, no. 3 (1999): 405–31.

45. Delwin Brown, *Boundaries of Our Habitations: Tradition and Theological Construction* (Albany: State University of New York Press, 1994), 90.

46. Karl Rahner, *On the Theology of Death*, trans. Charles H. Henkey (New York: Herder and Herder, 1961), 74.

Chapter 6. Toward Cosmic Wholeness

1. George L. Murphy, *The Cosmos in Light of the Cross* (Harrisburg, PA: Trinity Press International, 2003), 189.

2. Wolfhart Pannenberg, *Jesus—God and Man*, trans. Lewis L. Wilkins and Duane Priebe, 2nd ed. (Westminster, KY: John Knox Press, 1968), 67.

3. Ted Peters, *God: The World's Future*, 2nd ed. (Minneapolis: Fortress Press, 2000), 320.

4. Pierre Teilhard de Chardin, *Christianity and Evolution*, trans. René Hague (New York: Harcourt Brace and Co., 1969), 181.

5. *Pierre Teilhard de Chardin: Writings/Selected* (Maryknoll, NY: Orbis Books, 1999), 84.

6. Paul Tillich, *The New Being* (New York: Charles Scribner's Sons, 1955), 15.

7. Ibid., 16–18.

8. Ibid., 20–21.

9. Ken Wilber, *Up from Eden: A Transpersonal View of Human Evolution* (Wheaton, IL: Quest Books, 1996), 16.

10. Ray Kurzweil, quoted in Ashlee Vance, "Merely Human? That's So Yesterday," *New York Times* (June 11, 2010); available online.

11. Robert Jastrow, quoted in Theodore Roszak, "Evolution and the Transcendence of Mind," *Perspectives* 1, no. 2 (May 15, 1996); available online.

12. Ray Kurzweil, *The Age of Spiritual Machines: When Computers Exceed Human Intelligence* (New York: Viking, 1999), 3–5. Kurzweil defines the singularity as the point at which machines become sufficiently intelligent to start teaching themselves. When that happens, he says, the world will irrevocably shift from the biological to the mechanical. See also Robert Geraci, "Apocalyptic AI: Religion and the Promise of Artificial Intelligence," *Journal of the American Academy of Religion* 76, no. 1 (March 2008), 154.

13. Robert Geraci, "Spiritual Robots: Religion and Our Scientific View of the Natural World," *Theology and Science* 4, no. 3 (2006), 235.

14. Hans Moravec, *Mind Children: The Future of Robot and Human Intelligence* (Cambridge, MA: Harvard University Press, 1988), 1–2, 110–12.

15. Ibid., 4.

16. Daniel Crevier, *AI: The Tumultuous History of the Search for Artificial Intelligence* (New York: Basic Books, 1994), 278–80.

17. Antje Jackelén, "The Image of God as *Techno Sapiens*," *Zygon* 37, no. 2 (2002): 294.

18. Michael Heim, *The Metaphysics of Virtual Reality* (New York: Oxford University Press, 1993), 95; see also, David F. Noble, *The Religion of Technology: The Divinity of Man and the Spirit of Invention* (New York: Knopf, 1997), 159.

19. Michael Benedikt, ed., "Introduction," in *Cyberspace: First Steps* (Cambridge, MA: MIT, 1991), 16.

20. Geraci, "Apocalyptic AI," 165.

21. Tillich, *The New Being*, 24.

22. Zachary Hayes, "Christ, the Word of God and Exemplar of Humanity," *Cord* 46, no. 1 (1996): 12.

23. John F. Haught, personal communication.

24. Ronald Cole-Turner, "Biotechnology and the Religion-Science Discussion," in *The Oxford Handbook of Religion and Science*, ed. Philip Clayton and Zachary Simpson (New York: Oxford University Press, 2006), 941.

25. Ibid.

26. Ibid., 942.

27. See Michael W. Holmes, trans., "The Didache," in *The Apostolic Fathers*, rev. ed. (Grand Rapids, MI: Baker Books, 1999), 261.

28. Pierre Teilhard de Chardin, "The Mass on the World," in *Hymn of the Universe* (London: Collins, 1965), 24.

29. Denis Edwards, *Ecology at the Heart of Faith: The Change of the Heart that Leads to a New Way of Living on Earth* (Maryknoll, NY: Orbis Books, 2008), 106.

Chapter 7. Can the Church Evolve?

1. See Douglas Pratt, "Christian Discipleship and Interfaith Engagement," *Pacifica* 22 (October 2009): 317. Pratt notes that the British Council of Churches endorsed four principles of interfaith dialogue: dialogue begins when people meet each other; dialogue depends upon mutual understanding and mutual trust; dialogue makes it possible to share in service to the community; dialogue becomes the medium of authentic witness. See also Ilia Delio, *Christ in Evolution* (Maryknoll, NY: Orbis Books, 2008), 147–50.

2. Bonaventure shows a decided preference for the term *Word*, for this title signifies a complex network of relations that the Son bears to the Father, to creation, to humanity, and to revelation. The Son of the Father's love is simultaneously the Word of the Father's self-expression as loving, fruitful source of all that is. See Zachary Hayes, "Incarnation and Creation in St. Bonaventure," in *Studies Honoring Ignatius Brady, Friar Minor*, ed. Romano Stephen Almagno and Conrad L. Harkins (St. Bonaventure, NY: The Franciscan Institute, 1976), 314; Zachary Hayes, "The Meaning of *Convenientia* in the Metaphysics of St. Bonaventure," *Franciscan Studies* 34 (1974): 90.

3. "Reminders for Pilgrims and Strangers," *The Sermon Notebook: Biblical Resources for Preachers and Teachers of the Word of God!* Available on the www.sermonnotebook.org website.

4. Lynn White, "The Historical Roots of Our Ecologic Crisis," *Science* 155 (March 10, 1967): 1205.

5. Sandra M. Schneiders, "God So Loved the World . . . Ministerial Religious life in 2009," talk on vowed religious life given to the IHM Congregration, June 14, 2009), 22. Schneiders points out that "the Fourth Gospel uses the Greek word for world, 'kosmos,' 78 times, more than the rest of the New Testament put together."

6. Ibid., 23.

7. Ibid.

8. Ibid.

9. Ibid., 22–24.

10. Thomas Merton, *New Seeds of Contemplation* (New York: New Directions, 1961), 78, 79.

11. N. Max Wildiers, "Foreword," in Pierre Teilhard de Chardin, *Christianity and Evolution*, trans. René Hague (New York: Harcourt Brace and Co., 1969), 9.

12. Henri De Lubac, *Teilhard de Chardin: The Man and His Meaning*, trans. René Hague (New York: Hawthorn Books, 1965), 22.

13. Wildiers, "Foreword," 10.

14. Pierre Teilhard de Chardin, *Science and Christ*, trans. René Hague (New York: Harper and Row, 1968), 36; see also *Pierre Teilhard de Chardin: Writings/Selected* (Maryknoll, NY: Orbis Books, 1999), 92.

15. Pierre Teilhard de Chardin, *The Future of Man*, trans. Norman Denny (New York: Harper and Row, 1964), 309.

16. Pierre Teilhard de Chardin, *The Divine Milieu* (New York: Harper and Row, 1960), 69.

17. Ursula King, *Christ in All Things* (Maryknoll, NY: Orbis Books, 1997), 80.

18. Teilhard de Chardin, *Christianity and Evolution*, 93.

19. Pierre Teilhard de Chardin, *Toward the Future*, trans. René Hague (New York: Harcourt, 1975), 95.

20. Teilhard de Chardin, *Christianity and Evolution*, 91–92.

21. David Bohm, *Wholeness and the Implicate Order* (New York: Routledge and Kegan Paul, 1980), 124–25. See also William Stoeger, "What Does Science Say about Creation?" *The Month* (August/September 1988): 807.

22. Teilhard de Chardin, *Christianity and Evolution*, 49.

23. See N. T. Wright, *Surprised by Hope: Rethinking Heaven, the Resurrection, and the Mission of the Church* (New York: HarperOne, 2008), 18. Wright states: "God's kingdom in the preaching of Jesus refers not to post-mortem destiny, not to our escape from this world into another one, but to God's sovereign rule coming 'on earth as it is in heaven.'"

24. See, for example, Pierre Teilhard de Chardin, *The Phenomenon of Man*, trans. Bernard Wall (New York: Harper and Row, 1959), 53–57.

25. See John Milbank, *Theology and Social Theory: Beyond Secular Reason*, 2nd ed. (Oxford: Blackwell, 2006), 15, 27, 55. Milbank sees modernity and the secular sphere as an outcome of theology, and focus on John Duns Scotus' doctrine of univocity as a principal influence on the rise of modernity. See also Amos Funkenstein, *Theology and the Scientific Imagination* (Princeton, NJ: Princeton University Press, 1989), 25–31, 54–59.

26. Ultramontanism, in Roman Catholicism, refers to the belief in the superiority of papal authority over the authority of any other body or title holder, including the local bishop or a conference of bishops. See Frederick J. Cwiekowski, "Ultramontanism," in *Dictionary of Theology*, ed. Joseph A. Komonchak, Mary Collins, and Dermot A. Lane (Wilmington, DE: Michael Glazier, 1987), 1064.

27. In a 2008 study on religious affiliation by the Pew Forum on Religion and Public Life, 28 percent of all Americans reported that they have either changed religious affiliation or claim no formal religion at all. According to this study the Catholic Church has been hardest hit, with a 10 percent loss of members. This loss has been offset, however, by the number of Catholic immigrants. Jesuit Father Allan Figueroa Deck, executive director of the U.S. Bishops' Secretariat of Cultural Diversity in the Church, said that the trend of adult Catholics leaving the church points to the "lack of a more vigorous engagement" with the church's diverse membership (quoted in Carol Zimmerman, "Drop in Number of U.S. Catholics Offset by New Immigrants, Study Says," Catholic News Service, February 2008, online).

28. Devolution is symptomatic of Platonic metaphysics. In Plotinus's philosophy of emanation, for example, all things flow from the One; thus, the occurrence of new things takes place as *devolution*, as a thinning out of the power of being that resides in the divine principle prior to the process of creation. That is, emanation from the One is a sharing of being in such a way that created being derives being from Being and hence participates in Being without becoming something new. See Ilia Delio, "Godhead or God Ahead? Rethinking the Trinity in Light of Emergence," in *God, Grace and Creation*, ed. Philip J. Rossi, vol. 55, College Theology Society (Maryknoll, NY: Orbis Books, 2010), 7.

29. Charles M. Sennott, "Catholic Church Withers in Europe," *Boston Globe* (May 2, 2005); available online.

Chapter 8. The Inner Universe

1. Raimon Panikkar, *Christophany: The Fullness of Man*, trans. Alfred DiLascia (Maryknoll, NY: Orbis Books, 2004), 122.

2. Ibid., 124.

3. Hans Urs von Balthasar, "Bonaventure," in *The Glory of the Lord: A Theological Aesthetics*, vol. 2, *Studies in Theological Style: Clerical Styles*, trans. Andrew Louth, Francis McDonagh, and Brian McNeil, ed. John Riches (San Franciso: Ignatius Press, 1984), 356.

4. Jürgen Moltmann, *The Crucified God: The Cross of Christ as the Foundation and Criticism of Christian Theology*, trans. R. A. Wilson and John Bowden (New York: HarperCollins, 1991), 205.

5. Walter Kasper, *The God of Jesus Christ*, trans. Matthew J. O'Connell (New York: Crossroad, 1999), 195.

6. Dietrich Bonhoeffer, *Letters and Papers from Prison*, ed. Eberhard Bethge (London: Macmillan, 1972), 360.

7. Moltmann, *Crucified God*, 254.

8. Bonaventure, *Soliloquium* 1.39 (VIII 41). English translation by José de Vinck, *Soliloquy*, vol. 2, *Mystical Opuscula* (Paterson, NJ: St. Anthony Guild Press, 1966), 69.

9. Kenneth and Michael Himes, "The Sacrament of Creation," *Commonweal* (January 26, 1990): 45.

10. Thomas Merton, *New Seeds of Contemplation* (New York: New Directions, 1961), 16–17.

11. Himes and Himes, "The Sacrament of Creation," 45.

12. Colin E. Gunton, *The Triune God: A Historical and Systematic Study* (Grand Rapids, MI: Eerdmans, 1998), 65–96; cf. Jürgen Moltmann, *God in Creation: A New Theology of Creation and the Spirit of God*, trans. Margaret Kohl (Minneapolis: Fortress Press, 1993): "The formula *creatio ex nihilo* is an exclusive formula. The word *nihil* is a limit concept: out of nothing—that is to say out of pure nothingness. The preposition 'out of' does not point to any pre-given thing; it excludes matter of any kind whatsoever" (74).

13. Himes and Himes, "The Sacrament of Creation," 45.

14. Barbara Fiand, *Living the Vision: Religious Vows in an Age of Change* (New York: Crossroad, 1990), 59.

15. Leonardo Boff, *St. Francis: A Model for Human Liberation* (Maryknoll, NY: Orbis Books, 2006), 39.

16. Bonaventure, "The Life of Saint Francis," in *Bonaventure: The Soul's Journey into God, The Tree of Life, The Major Life of Saint Francis*, trans. Ewert H. Cousins, Classics of Western Spirituality (New York: Paulist Press, 1978), 254–55; Himes and Himes, *Fullness of Faith*, 119.

17. Himes and Himes, "The Sacrament of Creation," 45.

18. Bonaventure, in *Bonaventure* (Cousins translation), 55.

19. Merton, *New Seeds of Contemplation*, 34.

20. Barbara Fiand, *Releasement: Spirituality for Ministry* (New York: Crossroad, 1987), 26.

21. Gerard Manley Hopkins, "God's Grandeur" (1877); available online.

22. Gerard Manley Hopkins, "As Kingfishers Catch Fire" (before 1883); available online.

23. Kathleen Norris, *The Quotidian Mysteries: Laundry, Liturgy, and "Women's Work"* (New York: Paulist Press, 1998), 10.

24. Richard R. Gaillardetz, *Transforming Our Days: Spirituality, Community, and Liturgy in a Technological Culture* (New York: Crossroad, 2000), 67.

25. See, for example, Leonardo Boff, *Cry of the Earth, Cry of the Poor* (Maryknoll, NY: Orbis Books, 1997; originally published in Brazil, 1995).

26. Rainer Maria Rilke, "The Buddha in Glory" (1908); available online.

27. Bonaventure, in *Bonaventure* (Cousins translation), 116.

28. Ibid., 115

29. Cyprian Smith, *The Way of Paradox: Spiritual Life as Taught by Meister Eckhart* (Mahwah, NJ: Paulist Press, 1987), cited in John Shea, *Following Jesus* (Maryknoll, NY: Orbis Books, 2010), 60 61.

30. Bonaventure, *Collations on the Six Days of Creation*, trans. José de Vinck (Paterson, NJ: St. Anthony Guild Press, 1971), 39.

31. For Bonaventure, *perscrutatio* means allowing the depth of the mystery to unveil itself without destroying it. The theologian who is a *perscrutator* is like a treasure hunter—a seeker of pearls—who fathoms the unsuspected depths of the divine mystery, searching out its inmost hiding places and revealing its most beautiful jewels. Bonaventure indicates that when God expresses something of his trinitarian grandeur, it is then left to the theologian to search it out or penetrate it insofar as one allows oneself to be inhabited by the wisdom of God, which alone brings all things to light. See Emmanuel Falque, "The Phenomenological Act of *Perscrutatio* in the Proemium of St. Bonaventure's Commentary on the Sentences," trans. Elisa Mangina, in *Medieval Philosophy and Theology* 10 (2001): 9–18.

32. Bonaventure, *Collations on the Six Days of Creation*, 37.

33. Ibid., 37.

34. Ilia Delio, "Theology, Metaphysics, and the Centrality of Christ," *Theological Studies* 68, no. 2 (2007): 270–71.

35. Francis of Assisi, "Canticle of the Creatures," in *Francis of Assisi: Early Documents*, vol. 1, *The Saint*, ed. Regis J. Armstrong, J. A. Wayne Hellmann, and William J. Short (New York: New City Press, 1999), 114.

36. Ronald Rolheiser, *The Holy Longing: The Search for a Christian Spirituality* (New York: Doubleday, 1999), 9.

37. Beatrice Bruteau, *The Grand Option: Personal Transformation and a New Creation* (Notre Dame, IN: University of Notre Dame Press, 2001), 129–30. For a good discussion on Teilhard's mysticism and christogenesis, see Martin S. Laird, "The Diaphanous Universe: Mysticism in the Thought of Pierre Teilhard de Chardin," *Studies in Spirituality* 4 (1994): 206–35; Ursula King, "'Consumed by Fire from Within': Teilhard de Chardin's

Panchristic Mysticism in Relation to the Catholic Tradition," *Heythrop Journal* 40 (1999): 456–77.

38. George A. Maloney, *The Cosmic Christ: From Paul to Teilhard* (New York: Sheed and Ward, 1968), 189. See also N. Max Wildiers, *The Theologian and His Universe: Theology and Cosmology from the Middle Ages to the Present* (New York: Seabury Press, 1982), 207. Wildiers writes: "The completion of the world in Christ is not imposed on us as a necessity but is offered to us as a possibility that will not be realized without our cooperation. The further evolution of humankind ought to be our main concern."

Chapter 9. Christ the Living One

1. Bonaventure III *Sent.* d. 32, q. 5, ad 3 (III, 706).

2. Pierre Teilhard de Chardin, *The Phenomenon of Man*, trans. Bernard Wall (New York: Harper and Row, 1959), 293–94; Timothy Jamison, "The Personalized Universe of Teilhard de Chardin," in *There Shall Be One Christ*, ed. Michael Meilach (New York: The Franciscan Institute, 1968), 26.

3. Barbara Taylor Brown, "Physics and the Faith: The Luminous Web," *Christian Century* (June 2–9, 1999): 613.

4. Charles Taylor, *A Secular Age* (Cambridge, MA: Belknap Press, 2007), 299.

5. Ibid., 173.

6. Ewert H. Cousins, "Teilhard's Concept of Religion and the Religious Phenomenon of Our Time," *Teilhard Studies* 49 (Fall 2004): 13.

7. Elizabeth Gilbert, *Eat, Pray, Love: One Woman's Search for Everything across Italy, India, and Indonesia* (New York: Penguin Books, 2007), 54.

8. Ibid., 185, 208.

9. Ibid., 328.

10. For a discussion of chaos theory see James Glieck, *Chaos: Making a New Science* (New York: Penguin Books, 2008); Ilya Prigogene and Isabella Stenger, *Order Out of Chaos* (Boston: Shambhala Publications, 1984).

11. Francis of Assisi, "Admonition 6.3," in *Francis of Assisi: Early Documents*, vol. 1, *The Saint*, ed. Regis J. Armstrong, J. A. Wayne Hellmann, and William J. Short (New York: New City Press, 1999), 131.

12. Taylor Brown, "Physics and Faith," 614.

13. Maloney, *The Cosmic Christ*, 211.

14. Harvey D. Egan, "A Rahnerian Response to *Dominus Jesus*," *Australian EJournal of Theology* 2 (February 2004); available online.

15. Simone Weil, *Gravity and Grace*, trans. Arthur Wills (Lincoln: University of Nebraska, 1997), 132.

16. Pierre Teilhard de Chardin, *The Future of Man*, trans. Norman Denny (New York: Harper and Row, 1964), 309.

17. *Pierre Teilhard de Chardin*, writings selected with an introduction by Ursula King (Maryknoll, NY: Orbis Books, 1999), 124.

18. Ursula King, *Christ in All Things* (Maryknoll, NY: Orbis Books, 1997), 93.

19. Pierre Teilhard de Chardin, *Christianity and Evolution*, trans. René Hague (New York: Harcourt Brace and Co., 1969), 93.

20. Ibid., 170, 49.

21. Beatrice Bruteau, *The Holy Thursday Revolution* (Maryknoll, NY: Orbis Books, 2005).

22. Beatrice Bruteau, *The Grand Option: Personal Transformation and a New Creation* (Notre Dame, IN: University of Notre Dame Press, 2001), 172.

23. Denis Edwards, *Jesus and the Cosmos* (New York: Paulist Press, 1991), 66.

24. Ibid., 93.

25. Bruteau, *The Grand Option*, 172–73.

Conclusion

1. Karl Rahner, *Foundations of Christian Faith: An Introduction to the Idea of Christianity*, trans. William V. Dych (New York: Seabury Press, 1978), 197.

2. John F. Haught, *Responses to 101 Questions on God and Evolution* (Mahwah, NJ: Paulist Press, 2001), 136.

Glossary

Anthropic principle: The principle that states that, since humans are known to exist, the laws of physics must be such that life can exist. The strong version of the anthropic principle states that the universe has been designed for (human) life. The weak version says that conditions were just right in a part of the universe for carbon-based life to appear.

Big Bang model: The currently accepted model of the universe, according to which time and space emerged from a hot, dense, compact region about 13.7 billion years ago.

Black hole: A region of space whose immense, dense gravitational field traps anything, even light, that gets too close (closer than the black hole's event horizon).

Classical physics: The physical laws of Newton and Maxwell. The term is generally used to refer to all nonquantum laws of physics, including special and general relativity.

Cosmology: The study of the origin and evolution of the universe.

Cosmic microwave background radiation (CMB): A pervasive "sea" of electromagnetic radiation (photons) emanating almost uniformly from every direction in the universe, which dates back to the moment of recombination. This radiation, detected by Arno Penzias and Robert Wilson in 1965, is the "echo" of the Big Bang.

Cosmos: The entire universe.

Dark matter: A postulated form of matter, believed to make up a significant fraction of the matter in the universe. It makes its presence felt by its gravity, but it emits little or no visible light.

Ecology: From the Greek *oikos* ("household"), the study of the earth "household," more specifically, the relationships that interlink all members of the earth.

Emergence: The way complex systems and patterns arise out of a multiplicity of relatively simple interactions. Emergence points to novelty in nature that cannot be reduced to their sum or their difference from previous forms or systems.

Entropy: A measure of the disorder of a physical system; the number of rearrangements of a system's fundamental constituents that leave its gross overall appearance unchanged.

Entanglement: Quantum phenomenon in which spatially distant particles have correlated properties; unmediated action at a distance. A nonlocal interaction links one location with another without crossing space, without decay, and without delay.

Evolution: The process of development into different and generally more complex and fit forms.

Field: A "mist" or "essence" permeating space; it can convey an unseen force or describe the presence/motion of particles. Mathematically, a field involves a number or collection of numbers at each point in space, signifying the field's value.

General relativity: Einstein's theory of gravity, which invokes curvature of space and time.

Holon: Something that is simultaneously a whole and a part; a whole that is part of other wholes. Holons develop with increasing complexity.

Implicate order: A way of looking at reality not merely in terms of external interactions among things, but in terms of the internal (enfolded) relationships among things; undivided wholeness in flowing movement.

Inertia: Property of an object that resists acceleration.

Milky Way: A name given to the galaxy in which our solar system resides. The Milky Way is a spiral galaxy containing around 200 billion stars. The sun is located in one of its spiral arms.

Model: A self-consistent set of rules and parameters intended to describe mathematically some aspect of the real world.

Morphogenetic field: Unseen forces that preserve the form of self-organizing systems by maintaining order from within.

Observable universe: The part of the universe within our cosmic horizon; the part of the universe close enough so that light emitted can have reached us by today; the part of the universe we can see.

Photon: An elementary particle, the quantum of the electromagnetic interaction; the basic unit of light and all other forms of electromagnetic radiation.

Quanta: The minimum units of physical entities involved in an interaction; an entity that is "quantized" is the energy transfer of elementary particles of matter (called fermions) and of photons and other bosons. The word comes from the Latin *quantus*, meaning "how much."

Quantum mechanics: The theory, developed in the 1920s and 1930s, that describes the realm of atoms and subatomic particles.

Red shift: In cosmology this term is usually associated with the stretching of light waves from a distant galaxy as the universe expands. The galaxy is not receding through space, but the expansion of space itself is causing the red shift.

Self-Organizing System: A form or structure that maintains itself from within.

Singularity: The super-dense particle at the core of a black hole, or the location where the quantities that are used to measure the gravitational field become infinite in a way that does not depend on the coordinate system. Singularities can be divided according to whether they are covered by an event horizon or not (naked singularities). According to general relativity, the initial state of the universe, at the beginning of the Big Bang, was a singularity.

System: An integrated whole whose essential properties arise from the relationships among its parts.

Uncertainty principle: Property of quantum mechanics in which there is a fundamental limit on how precisely certain complementary physical features can be measured or specified.

Web of life: Interacting network organization of living organisms.

Selected Bibliography

Bohm, David. *Wholeness and the Implicate Order.* New York: Routledge and Kegan Paul, 1980.

Bracken, Joseph A. *Subjectivity, Objectivity, and Intersubjectivity.* West Conshohocken, PA: Templeton Foundation Press, 2009.

Brown, Barbara Taylor. *The Luminous Web: Essays on Science and Religion.* Boston, MA: Cowley Publications, 2000.

Bruteau, Beatrice. *Evolution toward Divinity: Teilhard de Chardin and the Hindu Traditions.* Wheaton, IL: The Theosophical Publishing House, 1974.

———. *The Grand Option: Personal Transformation and a New Creation.* Notre Dame, IN: University of Notre Dame Press, 2001.

Cannato, Judy. *Radical Amazement: Contemplative Lessons from Black Holes, Supernovas, and Other Wonders of the Universe.* Notre Dame, IN: Sorin Books, 2006.

———. *Fields of Compassion: How the New Cosmology Is Transforming Spiritual Life.* Notre Dame, IN: Sorin Books, 2010.

Capra, Fritjof. *The Tao of Physics.* New York: Bantam Books, 1984.

———. *The Web of Life: A New Scientific Understanding of Living Systems.* New York: Doubleday, 2006.

Clayton, Philip. *Mind and Emergence: From Quantum to Consciousness.* New York: Oxford University Press, 2004.

Clayton, Philip, and Arthur Peacocke, eds. *In Him We Live and Move and Have Our Being: Panentheistic Reflections on God's Presence in a Scientific World.* Grand Rapids, MI: Eerdmans, 2004.

Clayton, Philip, and Zachary Simpson, eds. *The Oxford Handbook of Religion and Science.* New York: Oxford University Press, 2006.

Collins, Francis S. *The Language of God: A Scientist Presents Evidence for Belief.* New York: Free Press, 2006.

Cousins, Ewert H., ed. *Process Theology: Basic Writings.* New York: Newman Press, 1971.

Delio, Ilia. *Christ in Evolution.* Maryknoll, NY: Orbis Books, 2008.

De Lubac, Henri. *Teilhard de Chardin: The Man and His Meaning.* Translated by René Hague. New York: Hawthorn Books, 1965.

Edwards, Denis. *Jesus and the Cosmos*. New York: Paulist Press, 1991.

———. *The God of Evolution*. New York: Paulist Press, 1999.

———. *Breath of Life: A Theology of the Creator Spirit*. Maryknoll, NY: Orbis Books, 2004.

———. *Ecology at the Heart of Faith: The Change of the Heart That Leads to a New Way of Living on Earth*. Maryknoll, NY: Orbis Books, 2008.

———. *How God Acts: Creation, Redemption, and Special Divine Action*. Minneapolis: Fortress Press, 2010.

Frank, Adam. *The Constant Fire: Beyond the Science vs. Religion Debate*. Berkeley and Los Angeles: University of California Press, 2009.

Greene, Brian. *The Fabric of the Cosmos: Space, Time, and the Texture of Reality*. New York: Vintage Books, 2004.

Hathaway Mark and Leonardo Boff. *The Tao of Liberation: Exploring the Ecology of Transformation*. Maryknoll, NY: Orbis Books, 2009.

Haughey, John, SJ. *Where Is Knowing Going? The Horizons of the Knowing Subject*. Washington, DC: Georgetown University Press, 2009.

Haught, John F. *God after Darwin: A Theology of Evolution*. Boulder, CO: Westview Press, 2000.

———. *Responses to 101 Questions on God and Evolution*. Mahwah, NJ: Paulist Press, 2001.

———. *Deeper Than Darwin*. Boulder, CO: Westview Press, 2003.

———. *Is Nature Enough? Meaning and Truth in the Age of Science*. New York: Cambridge University Press, 2006.

———. *Making Sense of Evolution: Darwin, God, and the Drama of Life*. Louisville, KY: Westminster John Knox Press, 2010.

Kelly, J. N. D. *Early Christian Doctrine*. New York: Harper and Row, 1978.

King, Ursula. *Christ in All Things*. Maryknoll, NY: Orbis Books, 1997.

Kurzweil, Ray. *The Age of Spiritual Machines: When Computers Exceed Human Intelligence*. New York: Penguin Books, 1999.

Maloney, George A. *The Cosmic Christ: From Paul to Teilhard*. New York: Sheed and Ward, 1968.

Miller, James. *An Evolving Dialogue: Theological and Scientific Perspectives on Evolution*. Harrisburg, PA: Trinity Press International, 2001.

Mooney, Christopher F., SJ. *Teilhard de Chardin and the Mystery of Christ*. New York: Harper and Row, 1966.

Moravec, Hans. *Mind Children: The Future of Robot and Human Intelligence*. Cambridge, MA: Harvard University Press, 1988.

Murphy, George L. *The Cosmos in Light of the Cross*. Harrisburg, PA: Trinity Press International, 2003.

Noble, David F. *The Religion of Technology: The Divinity of Man and the Spirit of Invention*. New York: Knopf, 1997.

O'Murchu, Diarmuid. *Ancestral Grace: Meeting God in Our Human Story*. Maryknoll, NY: Orbis Books, 2008.

Panikkar, Raimon. *Christophany: The Fullness of Man*. Translated by Alfred DiLascia. Maryknoll, NY: Orbis Books, 2004.

Pannenberg, Wolfart.*Theology and the Kingdom of God*. Edited by Richard John Neuhaus. Philadelphia: Westminster Press, 1977

Peters, Ted. *God: The World's Future*. Minneapolis: Fortress Press, 2000.

Polkinghorne, John, ed. *The Work of Love: Creation as Kenosis*. Grand Rapids, MI: Eerdmans, 2001.

Rahner, Karl. *On the Theology of Death*. Translated by Charles H. Henkey. New York: Herder and Herder, 1961.

Sheldrake, Rupert. *The Presence of the Past: Morphic Resonance and the Habits of Nature*. Rochester, VT: Park Street Press, 1995.

———. *Morphic Resonance: The Nature of Formative Causation*. Rochester, VT: Park Stree Press, 2009.

Singh, Simon. *Big Bang: The Origin of the Universe*. New York: HarperCollins, 2004.

Shults, F. LeRon. *Christology and Science*. Grand Rapids, MI: Eerdmans, 2008.

Teilhard de Chardin, Pierre. *The Phenomenon of Man*. Translated by. Bernard Wall. New York: Harper and Row, 1959.

———. *The Future of Man*. Translated by Norman Denny. New York: Harper and Row, 1964.

———. *Science and Christ*. Translated by René Hague. New York: Harper and Row, 1968.

———. *The Divine Milieu: An Essay on the Interior Life*. Translated by William Collins. New York: Harper and Row, 1969.

———. *Christianity and Evolution*. Translated by René Hague. New York: Harcourt Brace and Co., 1969.

———. *Activation of Energy*. Translated by René Hague. New York: Harcourt Brace Jovanovich, 1970.

———. *Toward the Future*. Translated by René Hague. New York: Harcourt, 1975.

———. *Pierre Teilhard de Chardin*. Writings selected with an introduction by Ursula King. Maryknoll, NY: Orbis Books, 1999.

Thompson, William M. *Christ and Consciousness: Exploring Christ's Contribution to Human Consciousness: The Origins and Development of Christian Consciousness*. New York: Paulist Press, 1977.

Toolan, David. *At Home in the Cosmos*. Maryknoll, NY: Orbis Books, 2001.

Wheatley, Margaret. *Leadership and the New Science: Discovering Order in a Chaotic World*. San Francisco: Berrett-Koehler, 1992.

Whitehead, Alfred North. *Process and Reality*. Edited by David Ray Griffin and Donald W. Sherburne. New York: Free Press, 1978.

Wilber, Ken. *Up from Eden: A Transpersonal View of Human Evolution*. Wheaton, IL: Quest Books, 1996.

———. *A Theory of Everything*. Boston: Shambhala Publications, 2000.

———. *Sex, Ecology, Spirituality: The Spirit of Evolution*. Boston: Shambhala Publications, 2001.

Wildiers, N. Max. *The Theologian and His Universe: Theology and Cosmology from the Middle Ages to the Present*. New York: Seabury Press, 1982.

Wright, N. T. *Surprised by Hope: Rethinking Heaven, the Resurrection, and the Mission of the Church*. New York: HarperOne, 2008.

Zizioulas, John. *Being As Communion: Studies in Personhood and the Church*. New York: St. Vladimir's Seminary Press, 1985.

Index